Trials

OF

Amaranthine

KAILIE MARIE LYNN BILL

Publisher: Dyre House
Hardcover: 978-1-7386925-2-1
Paperback: 978-1-7386925-1-4
eBook: 978-1-7386925-0-7

Website: www.kailiebill.com
Kailie Bill

First Edition 2023

This book is a work of fiction. Any similarity between the characters and situations within its pages and places or persons, living or dead, is unintentional and coincidental.

Book Cover Design and Interior Formatting by 100Covers.
Cover artwork by ROCKHOPPER on fiverr.com

WORKS BY
KAILIE MARIE LYNN BILL

Poetry
Trials of Amaranthine

Fiction
The Extra Ordinary
Kaia the Centaur: Hero-In-Training

THANK YOU

*I would like to express my deepest of gratitude to the following for taking a
chance and helping me with my book:
Adam Sparkes
Francesco Tehrani
Russel Van Humbeck
Chris Chord
Ajay Bhalla
Polly J. Mordant*

*   *   *   *   *

*And a special thank you to my family for encouraging me and knowing
that I could do it:
My parents, Kerry and Bill Bill
My brother, Jordan Bill
My aunt, Buffy Bill
And my grandparents, Marie and Bill Bill*

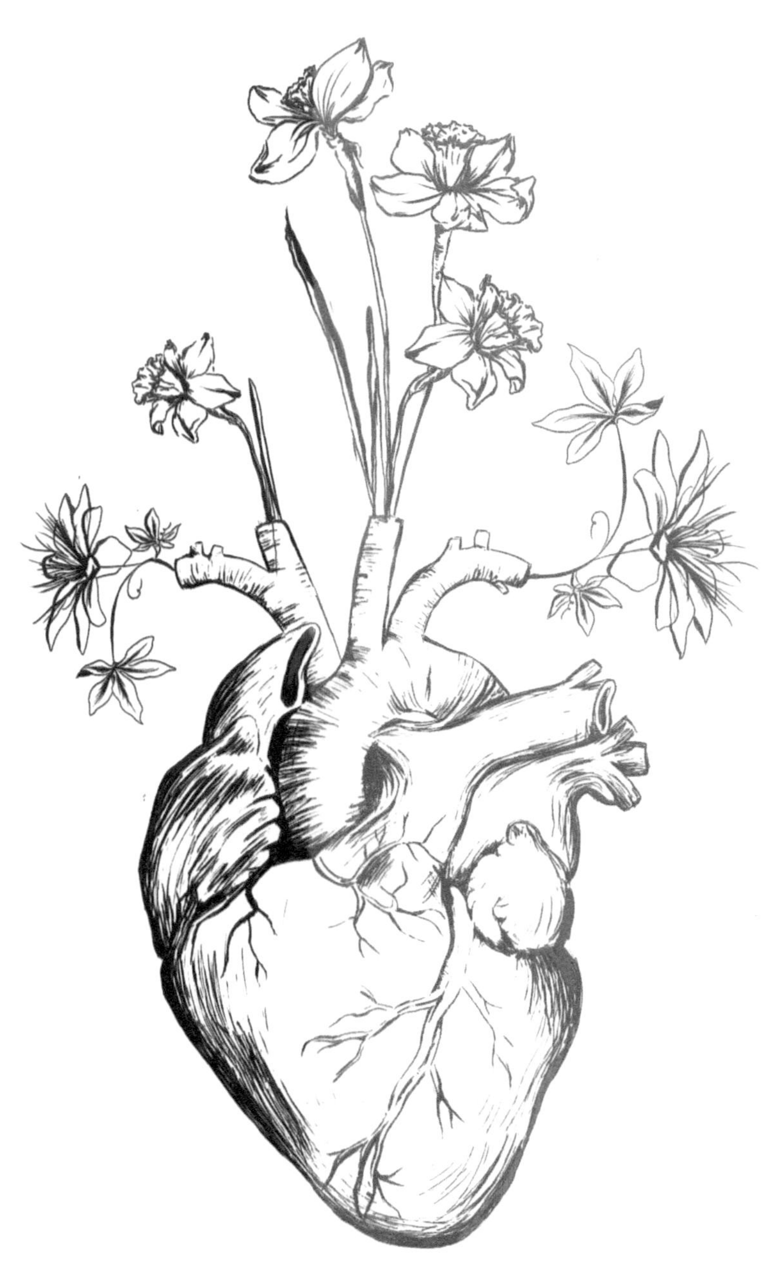

PROLOGUE

Visions of fire, of death, of fear, and of fright
Morsels to feed the black beast inside of him
Encouraging the tightening of the bight
With a silver-slicked tongue and voracious whim
Needle-toothed maw of decay piercing his head
Screams to light up the theatre's rotting scrim
No matter the distance gained, her face of dread—
Haunts the images swimming amongst his thoughts
Their babe son nestled to her breast on Death's bed
Running from invaders, their spears, and ersatz—
Claims to his rightful place of sanctuary
Blistering inferno blazing on love's knot

Then she was caught, shrieks for the Virgin Mary
Their dying son's weak cries echoing her fate
Doomed to the wishes of their adversary
To be killed at once without grace or debate
Or even worse for her, beauty's avatar
To be the top offering to the slave state
Hell's hall aflame, wood supports licked to black char
Heat enough to melt a man's courage and grit

Even to him, the most resolute by far
Still, the brave man reached for them, would not submit
Between the debris of the fallen ceiling
Cut off from his wife and child, he would not quit
Cursing the heavy smoke that was concealing—
His love and child. Her lips find his through the ash
A joyous touch, Heaven-sent, this pure feeling

"Go now, my king. I fear not a single lash
Our son has already passed. I will follow
Promise me you will live, if I may be brash
Without you in it, the world will be hollow
I will keep the vile invaders' attention
You must escape and your pride you must swallow
Please, my king, nod to me your comprehension
So that I might go in peace with your blessing
Your family to begin our ascension."

She retrieved her dagger, freed of its dressing
Weaponry and formal dress, like a mixed bud
One last tender smile, second of caressing
Her hands rose to undo her gown's neck press stud
Ne'er surer of her choice granting him his life
Knife to her lithe throat, a drop of crimson blood
"Put us from your mind so you live without strife."
She spoke her last, still cradling their dead son
"Allow me this duty as your faithful wife
This foe's plot to kill you I will make undone
By allowing your freedom and giving hope
They do not realize this day you have won

And I will not become a slave girl to grope
Paraded to tarnish your reputation
For I would sooner find myself on the rope
Or stampeded to death by raging oxen
Twenty or thirty, each driving their hooves in
Their horns leading to my belly's serration
Pain will blind and paralyze, even deafen
My screams reaching our loving Father above
But that's preferable to their godless sin
Behold. This is my gift to you: life, my love
Now go from here, before my woman's nerve wains."

She finished her statement with a kiss and shove
Gone into the thick ash, his sanity strains
His heart cleaving in two for his son and wife
He cursed Krios and his treacherous campaigns
He would put the old commander to his knife
Krios to look him in the eye with goodwill
Then cause such embarrassment upon his life?
Krios on his horse at the mountain's foothill
Watching as his trebuchets collapse the keep
Dressed to the nines with his garish pomp and frill
But our quick-footed hero kept his head deep—
In shadows, so Krios was none the wiser
Toward cover of the urbs did this king creep

The inhabitants flee from the raging fire
Crying women ripped from their babes and children
By footmen with cruel eyes under their visor
More and more try to run, to remain hidden

Amongst bodies of the dead and the dying
Hiding from those that need help but guilt-ridden
Survival takes hold, keeping them from trying
Eyes wide shut to the gurgles of death around

Another one falls, slashed clean through, still vying
Irises darting through the chaos abound
Tears burning cheeks, nonsense pleas through bloodstained lips
Hidden and dying eyes lock without a sound
Realization and then the eyes eclipse
Gone to be the guest of the Son and Father
And leaving the rest to the apocalypse

These dead the king climbed over without falter
To be rid of this fouled place no longer his
Return to a life that lacks any bother
Thoughts of wine, women, and friendly war games whiz—
Through his mind at a rapid pace, only calm—
When he rushes through the screaming peasants. 'Tis—
A sight to see, this king silent as a psalm
No wide-eyed one could find him, shadow's cousin
Pride swelled in the serfs' hearts like a needed balm
Before they were struck by a sword so sudden
To witness their king making fools of the foe
'Fore they fed Krios' base horde, the glutton
Their simple lives could live past the killing blow
For him! For their king! Go, great king, to the wood!
Where you can lose those curs around the willow
Famous for its just camouflage of the good
Whose lush leaves shield every malevolent stare

An unwritten test for one's rise to sainthood
Here he burst through the clearing, heart of despair
Behind him, the coward soldiers that stayed back
Too afraid to join their brothers in their err
Shaking in their armour at the pressed attack
And from their foxholes they see him behind piles—
Of rubble and dead, slinking from shack to shack
Easy, they thought, quivering chins change to smiles

They cried out, "Look, a lone man! On him no sword."
So they emerged from their place hiding in aisles
    "Simple to leave our posts. That we can afford
    Strike down this runner who abandons his men
    His head will win us favour with our warlord
    But hold, no common man is this, look again
    The head is held high, despite the gravity
    The heavy weight of knowledge beyond our ken
    His eyes are clear of vulgar depravity
    No common man, but King Wrenfrey of this land!
    A proud illustration of regality
    Second son to the late king, a man so grand
    And his sublime queen with endless golden hair
    Both blessed by angels at the Father's command
    To give rise to a kingdom equal and fair
    Lucky to have it passed down to the sterling
    The very one before us we're to ensnare!"

And so they gave chase, their fresh weapons whirling
The chance at reparations now close at hand
Yet they wobble and cry out like a yearling

Their timorous yips proving their manhood's brand
These children in iron, a smart man would shun
But Krios was in need of any weak band

So before their last bits of nerve were undone
They found themselves in the willow's vast clearing
The strong trunk standing alone under the sun
The great king and his skill of persevering—
Are put to the test as the cur lot scour

But the just willow kept him from appearing
Unbeknownst to them as they search the bower
Where was he? Right? Left? Up above? Down below?
The dear Father was surely with him that hour
No creature of true evil could overthrow
God's influence resting in the roots and leaves
The power hidden in the weeping willow

But, please, no more. Enough of this, the king grieves
He straightened his cloak, his poise a masterwork
And stepped out to meet these ill-fated life-thieves

They met him with gasps and gulps, or their freed dirk
    "Revealing yourself when it's seven to one
    Where's the strategist to make men weep?" A smirk

    "My wife and son have died, my home overrun,"
This great king of ruins, his piece he must say
    "I ask that you let His divine will be done
    If God has decreed that today is my day

Then to be amongst the overwhelming love
That can only occur while under His sway
But what I would do before the mourning dove

Sings my song from deep within its feathered chest
Had I more time before venturing above
Start anew, continue my line. My new quest
Find a woman, demure and affectionate
A humble home built for children to infest
Good luck or graces? We shall ne'er question it
Our sons will become champions of the land
One at swordplay, one fast with the chariot
Another will build his own kingdom by hand
And when grey infects my beard, they will return
To see their great father off by His command
That is my plan but the thoughts are mine to yearn
Now let us end this with some civility
Our heavenly Father is not one to spurn."

He knelt down, his head held in humility
He waited for the strike to come for his neck
For the bittersweet touch of tranquillity
But when it never came, and he rose to check
Only to see the footmen blinded by tears
Stripped of all their dignity, left not a speck
Weapons and shields fell away, gone are the fears

One stepped forth to greet our king as an equal
He's unknown to our king, this man up in years
Too old to be of use in war, but gleeful—

To finally meet a proper warrior
    "Too long I've been surrounded by such people
    That for their small selves could not feel sorrier
    For these, I hesitate to call men, are naught—
    But tailors, farmers, or even quarriers
    No taste for lifeblood, victory, or onslaught
    Gah! As they hid, I yelled for God's punishment
    Such cowardice there. Their pride an afterthought
    But your prayer hit me with such replenishment
    Your words called me in and sung of my own hope
    Such reflection, I gasped in astonishment
    Do you see the degree of your verses' scope?
    Look upon the men's faces, see how they cry
    Their kinship personified walks a tightrope
    Across the long chasm where twin lions lie
    Their names being Loyalty and Allegiance—

    To Krios, our king, they don't wish to defy
    The lions' roar and snarl, forcing their credence
    Threatening their belief and understanding
    Trying to turn them away from this grievance
    But they see it now, your morals long-standing
    How could they cut down a fair man such as you?
    They can't do what the lions are demanding
    Go, before the rest of his forces come through
    Have your many sons and farm, wife and freedom
    You must escape, so your desires become true

None here will question the right to your Eden
Should any soul speak up now, I'd strike them down
Go now, king, flee this growing mausoleum."

Respect etched for this footman across his heart
Then he was gone, lost to these lands by sundown

Left behind, screams coil with fires' smoke as all play their part
Beholden bodies separated like works of art

CHAPTER 1

A journey on foot. A manhunt for his head
King Wrenfrey ventured to the town of Wortstath
No crown, but not forgetting the life he led

A newcomer to all, put off by his wrath
Cycling plans of vengeance broken by cries
Oh, why did God set him on this shameful path?
A test of faith, to sort the truth from the lies?
Oh, great and glorious Father up above
Forgive this tattered man for being unwise
Your children forget Your work is out of love

And none of them is more loved than good Wrenfrey
God hides him from Krios, who's unworthy of—
His Grace, and protecting him from the gainsay
Spread by the slanderers and rumourmongers
The townsfolk of Wortstath are quick to obey
Especially those with wide eyes, the youngers
Not been poisoned with doubt or apprehension
Simple to tell that inside their soul hungers
Midst them, the girls with beauty to ease tension

In the weary muscles and mind of our king
The couplings free of every contention
But he knew not to throw off his life's past sting
He spread himself thin, to kingdoms far abroad
Expecting help from others to be wellspring

But those kings, friends of our king! Nothing but frauds!
Audiences ignored or mocked by the court
Waved away like some common licentious bawd
Misery they showered upon him for sport
All but siccing their castle's ravenous beasts
Once blood brothers, now with evil they consort
Because of horned Krios their honour is fleeced
Dripping whispers corroding years of friendship
Foolishly lapping up the liar's grand feast
With blind trust they accept the Devil's courtship
Preferring honeyed words over heartfelt pleas
Their dead souls now firmly in his iron grip
Our king, though strong and fearless, fell to his knees
He tore his clothes over his lost dominion
In mourning for the land, its bushes and trees
The great town he wrestled into submission
The townsmen who dropped their eyes as he passed by
The taverns that were always stocked with women

His castle next. He loosed one man's hue and cry
His guaranteed claim, his by birthright, stolen
His home now the home of a wretched gadfly
Our King Wrenfrey reduced to a base stolon
Forced to dig through muck, break away from his life

While a new monster's belly became swollen—
With *his* food and *his* wine, Krios twists the knife

But the death of his queen is what struck a chord
With her at his side, he became the envy
Of all hot-blooded men, something he adored
The loveliness of her eyes made them frenzy
The movement of her delicate wrists was grace
Her voice was always quiet and used gently
If only he could take in that sublime face
Once more sorrowful over his rotten luck
A fairer woman he will never embrace
As he grieves, those are the thoughts that run amok
King with no kingdom to live as a pauper
To be a forgettable waste lost in muck
Denied from cities and villages proper
His lineage cut short, obliterated
No bride price to be paid with a bare coffer

Then his thoughts push away from devastated
By a shadow and its warmth on his shoulder
A young woman sits, her target located

She first found our king when the air grew colder
Lost in fearful unfamiliarity
Our king's strong body had begun to moulder
Seeing his state, she offered him charity
He declined out of his noble principle
But moved by his aura of regality
She begged, pleaded, on lunacy's pinnacle

And so, to save her frail sanity, he went
Thanking glorious God for His miracle

In her home, names were exchanged between laments
But to say he remembered would be a lie
He was not accustomed to the poor's accent
And in truth, he had plans to solidify

Things unimportant to his life's new grand scheme—
Couldn't obstruct the design in his mind's eye
An A was at her name's start, that it would seem
Not like a peasant's name would lead to ruin
He concerns himself with those royal bloodstreams

Yet here he sits, hoping his troubles loosen
But his mind is already packed to the brim
As the nameless girl joins his grief in union
She greets our perfect king by his pseudonym
    "Good morning, Frey. Fearing the day's beginning?
    Go to the church and listen to the priest's hymn
    The kind words of our Lord help all with sinning
    But if the heart's not heavy with sin, pray tell
    I'm known through Wortstath for skills of listening
    Allow me entry into your hardened shell
    To link our arms, fight your demons, together
    And give you relief, if only for a spell."

Wind dances her crimson hair amongst heather
Her peculiar eyes of grey pierce his cold heart
And loosen the organ's thick tightened tether

But our king would not let himself fall apart
Strong and courageous, oh how our man provides!

    "A stunning woman, you are. A work of art,"
Frey says to her amongst the rolling hillsides
    "No reason to speak to a waste like myself
    I'm naught. Sure to join the lowly suicides
    A rope to the neck, climb to the highest shelf

    Or my sword through my belly with one swift thrust
    Bleed as I bleed for my home, my commonwealth
    Lying in a pool of my fragmented trust
    Never to stain the eyes of our Creator
    Cursed to follow the ones of murder and lust
    The paths of the heretic and the traitor
    As our loving God condemns me to brimstone
    'GUTTED OF ALL IN LIFE. WORTHLESS TESTATOR'
    That's what will be written upon my tombstone
    Not my many feats or my humility
    But my one loss, which was no fault of my own
    Now I only hope for Death's tranquillity."

There he stops, before sorrow takes him again
He had to regain his sensibility
For this low-class girl with her intellect feign
Would never understand the intricacies
Her eagerness like a dog's, just like her brain
But he'd ne'er mock, for the aristocracies—
Need them to make the world go from day to night
A careful balance filled with intimacies

Still, it was fascinating to watch her fight
Patrician psyche against serf acumen
At last, her soft voice whispered through the daylight
 "That was quite a lot. Running from such ruin
  I dare not insult you with 'it'll get better'
  But know that such things remind us we're human
  Nor will I speak, like some clueless abettor
  'Sure am I, it's not near as bad as you say'
  For you do believe every word and letter
  My family's guest, once the world's castaway
  My heart has been breaking as it's observed you
  We know nothing of you still, but the name Frey
  With such a heavy burden I wish I knew
  My friend, maybe I can push away your shroud?
  If only your injured self would let me through
  Lean on me, Frey, and please, without being proud
  Despite your blood obviously running blue
  Your emotions are no reason to feel cowed."
She ends with a small smile, quite a lovely view

And the girl can tell he is of noble birth
Even with his precautions, she saw right through
Perchance, in that redhead, is something of worth
But perhaps all sheep can sense the wolf beyond
Like a great creature of God's beautiful Earth—
Stalks along the banks for a meal to abscond
Our king lifts a hand to brush her soft pink cheek
 "With your words, I find myself becoming fond
  Ne'er truer beauty has made my knees grow weak."

The woman grasps the trailing hand on her face
Her ashen eyes wide, she thinks it best to speak.
    "And to have such attention makes my heart race
    But most likely the voice of grief I hear now
    Such life's struggles long to rest in comfort's place

    Mystery-laced future heavy on the brow
    Like tides on a lake shore, let it wash over
    And not headstrong like waves against a ship's bow
    Your life won't always be that of a rover
    God permits, you can settle yourself in town
    Life as a farmer, trader, or a drover
    And I'll be there to guide you all the way down."

And our king's reminded of her ignorance
A man of his stature reduced to a clown?
Oh well, brains were really more of a hindrance

But before she could be dazed by his glory
A voice cuts through, rousing his belligerence
The old serf farmer, his face sagged and hoary
Out his calls carry, "My lord, people have come
    Travelling from some unknown territory
    Many days straight they walked, their feet going numb
    But forever faithful to their Majesty
    Warriors willing to go blind, deaf, and dumb
    What kingship they serve, what a man he must be
    How I wished for such humanity above
    And not treatment as a tolerated flea
    Oh, if there was something I could dispose of

It would be those things that gorge themselves on high
On the broken backs whose births lacked God's true love
Those monsters I can only sometimes descry
Make me recount my days with the javelins
When forced into their wars that always pass by
Now come see this group of loyal paladins
Listen, through them, to their great Excellency
Hear the words you've held with hard-bitten talons."

Our king, your mind's eye goes where only men see
To your humble heartfelt pleas for your friends' help
This man to be his kingdom's skeleton key
His enthusiasm is that of a whelp
Our king's composure was never a strong suit
Sure enough, if he spoke you'd hear a dog's yelp
So quick as he can, he puts dirt under boot
'Cross the hills to meet his rival's harrowing
And show Krios his vengeance was absolute

The province's chains are rattled, violent billowing
A shudder across the land of a life's winnowing

CHAPTER 2

Into the hovel that the poor call a home
Where the flooring is dirt, and worn down walls reign
Nothing around to deter the rats that roam
But now stands a sight to make our king's eyes rain
Five monstrous brutes stood, upon their heads a shroud
Black like their armour, weapons in the same vein
Hidden beneath their face veils yet they stand proud
Each two men thick and a man and a half tall
Such strength! Could Krios see the rising war cloud?

The leader steps forth, not removing his shawl
   "We call on Wrenfrey, old king of Triastein
   We travelled, never lacking the wherewithal
   Nor letting loose a single lament or whine
   Not even letting our fatigued minds waver
   As it would be an insult to our bloodline
   And to earn our Excellency's disfavour
   We would sooner ask God to banish our souls—
   To Hell than to disappoint our lives' saviour

We live our lives proud, sanctified with our roles
We're the Hand of our ever-reaching monarch
Our duty to all our Majesty controls
We were told of your name and said to embark
To carry a message of utmost import
Start at dawn's new light and remove any dark
As I speak you may have want to cut me short
But to hear my story's to hear the capstone
Listen and understand the forces you court

I fought in a war, for honour not my own
In a war of blood for blood, a single goal
From such wanton violence, one cannot atone
At the time, I stood tall with my darkened soul
None could hold me back, not my men nor my foes
A ravenous beast, but battle takes its toll

I pushed too far too fast when the others froze
My sword thirsty for the blood of a traitor
As I alone stormed the keep, I came to blows—
With the royal guard of the violator
Despite my rage, they were more than I could take
Stabbed, slashed, hacked through, I could see our Creator

To die for retribution with need to slake
To be nothing but another's anecdote
To hear the surrounding death, destruction's quake

But then a shriek, otherworld, life's antidote
All around, whirling like a demon driven

Madness. Screams to be listeners' final quote
Then it came, a wraith, sight like death had risen
Obscure eyes hollow of God's holy caress
Impossibly stretched red-drenched grin like ribbon
But most of all was an aura of promise
To which my adversaries abandoned me
Running for the hills, survival is lawless

And my own body was too broken to flee
I died a thousand times over as it came
The creature nearing, pushing through the debris
Satan himself come to demonstrate his fame
My heart stilled as the thing, now by my side, knelt
Close to my ear, it whispered to me my name

And the voice was the most gut-wrenching sound dealt
Lips stayed shut, out of the red-drenched grin words rang
Teeth grinding metal, nails on slate, what I felt
My ears hissed, brimming with regret's pallid pang
Yet as it spoke, the more familiar it grew
Until I could only follow as it sang
I rose from my grave, my rent body anew
My wounds no more, my broken spirit returned
Most of all, sense of purpose I felt renew
The quiet ceremony, a new life earned
To ones you see before you and many more
A similar story for all who were burned
And so you hear my tale, king, what lies before
We come to ensure our Majesty's will's done
To give a choice and tempt with what you adore."

Listening to this brotherhood's story spun
Our revered king nearly collapses and weeps
For his cup of good fortune is overrun
He knew a king would wake from traitorous sleeps
But the name to who this man speaks escapes thought
And of the man's description where vileness seeps?
Corpse come to life? Evil's true face? Hell's mascot?
Common for the common man to be confused
When faced with those of visible higher wrought
Times our king would often find himself amused
At the silly stories, his town would whisper

But offers of support would not be refused
Demon or not, he cares not for the lisper
Men are what is needed, our king at the helm
He'll doom Krios from his horde to his sister!
All who dared to defile our king's august realm
With fire in his belly, our great king speaks thus:
    "Do all the men stand like you, strong as an elm?
    Bowing heads in loyalty without a fuss?
    Pray tell, do the men believe in their sovereign
    Placing upon their hand a devoted buss
    If so, you have found King Wrenfrey, not fallen
    I stand before you now ready to command
    The coming fight will never be forgotten."

But the warrior holds up his massive hand
His masked face still betraying nothing humane
    "Our Majesty plans a thorough reprimand

Upon that which has tormented your domain
Our long journey to you was but the first step
Next is to meet in our Excellency's plane
There, battle plans will be laid out for each prep
Our black seraph will make sure nothing slips past
As armies stalk across the expansive steppe
But you first must come meet our iconoclast
Standing before, face-to-face as peer-to-peer
Do this, King Wrenfrey, and the take shall be vast."

Such revelations make the farmer's eyes clear
Once a silent presence in the corner, strait
He grasps for our king, out of respect and fear
His decrepit bones no longer hold his weight
Upon hearing his guest's true identity
He falls to the floor, legs behind him, prostrate
    "How I see, my life is an obscenity
    A ragged man appears, and we take him in
    Now I pray for that ragged man's lenity
    Words that were spoken when I believed us kin
    A brashness had overcome me, Your Highness
    Now haunted by undeniable chagrin!"

The old peasant continues on his crisis
Pulling at our king's cloak with tears in his eyes
But our king is both merciful and righteous
He lifts his hand, hushing the troubled man's cries
    "Fear not, your inappropriate words and deeds
    For a good king cares for all, even the flies
    Gift me the three cows in your field for my needs

A celebration to a new alliance
Party for all until everyone fatigues
Old serf, I'll need your absolute compliance
Fetch the barley from your stores, the wheat as well
From my new friends, I expect no defiance
We shall rejoice, relax, let our bellies swell
With this, I shall always remember your name."

The old peasant swoons as he's spared Death's cold knell
And he rushes to obey his better's aim
As his betters remain to plan future goals
For the God-given right of our king's true fame

Silence of the country spreads thick over people's souls
Peeking, breaths quivering, like a child's gaze through keyholes

CHAPTER 3

Meat and ale abundant through Wortstath proper
All around the village people thank our king
All enjoy, from official to sharecropper
Women from all stations come to dance and sing
The torches' flames following their writhing hips
Brightening their skin as sweat struggles to cling
Their eyes hooded, tongues peek out to dab plump lips
Revealing their wanton temptresses within
So many tools they use to turn on their tricks

So little cloth for his fingers to unpin
A man would have to be dead to not enjoy
And yet the five shrouds stand, all a statue's twin
Waving off advances like some altar boy
Could it be their ruler denies them the right?
That was sure to change under our king's employ

Pulled from thought, he's met by a beautiful sprite
The serf's brood in a dress as simple as her
She drops into a curtsey, her face contrite
    "Frey, or now king? I know only how things were

Man of tatters presented as a true lord
As we helped you, I now ask for your succour
And please, between us keep this discussion stored
My father is a proud man, but also poor
He cares for me while his own needs go ignored
But asking for help is something he'd abhor
For a man is no man if his family—
Feels hunger's cruel pangs while he's full to his core
They ought to grow fat as he becomes gangly

At least, those are the words that escape his mouth
No matter what I say or think how silly
He acted like we were in a constant drouth
Forgive me, words fall from my lips without thought."
She gives a nervous grin to her lack of couth
But then her hands wring as her smile becomes fraught
    "Our cows, wheat, and barley, all proceeds to you
    Your contentment in all things is what we sought
    A deed for every person whose life's askew
    For we knew what it was like to be luckless
    But now, with this party, our own stores are few…"

Her face is open, honest, her cheeks bloodless
The girl attempts a warrior's confidence
But a cursory glance says she is gutless
Before our noble king with her commonness
She pulls in breath, bosom stretching her corset
A test of our exalted king's continence?
    "I come not asking where your loyalties sit
    Hope just blooms with thought you might return the boon

But asking a guest in shame, I won't force it
There will be no food for my frail father soon
I beseech, 'fore the return of winter's snow
In good faith, sing here a charitable tune
My father's shelves restocked with what you bestow
Nothing more I ask for, my lord, nothing more
Except for an answer. That I want to know."

Her words, her voice, lacks any sort of uproar
Authority too much for this gentle pearl
How it pierces his heart, desire to adore
Our grand protector grabs his cloak to unfurl
Around her angelic frame, he rests the cloth
Arm 'cross her shoulders, tickled by her hair's curl
Her eyelashes flicker like wings on a moth
He lifts her chin, exposing her moonlit throat
Lips near touching, like a lover's silent troth
Our Wrenfrey speaks, "Turn from trepidation's note
    A new provider—saviour!—encases you
    Gentle caress carries on your echoed troat
    Hear the hammering inside my breast anew
    Collapse into my arms and never have need
    Just want shall frequent. Give voice and I give two
    Come with me, to where I can answer your plead
    Out of view and heavy cloth that tends to itch
    Let us properly discuss what's been agreed."

The girl gazes as if his voice could bewitch
His body pressed to hers, their breaths mingling

As much fight in her body as some brat's lich
His head comes down to claim, his lips tingling

But only air greets him as his paramour
    "Frey—King, it seems your mind's daze is lingering
    Confusion about my wish at your mind's fore
    Mayhap my anxious words were ill-selected
    I ask for a refill of my father's store
    So he is fed, and his worry corrected
    It is not that I wish his body able
    So that *my* life is tended and protected
    But your offer, like a prince from a fable—
    Is suited to your grand personality
    Enough to make a woman's sense disable."

Our great king scarcely holds his carnality
The shadows pulling the corners of his smile
The words spoken by the commonality
Shock of rejection was enough to beguile
And all the more, his predator's soul hungers
Appetence for her heart spurs his new trial
He'll labour hard. Show wonders after wonders
Ah, women. They are truly the woe of men
And all the more ambrosial when he plunders
Our king, great thesp, is anything beyond ken?

He pastes on a face of convincing defeat
He's played this game with their kind time and again
Won't be long 'fore they're embraced in fervent heat
    "My girl, your words of wisdom are too exact

I expect your harshest and will not retreat
I have smudged your honour with my lack of tact
Allow me the chance to earn your forgiveness
I only wish for friendship to stay intact
It's not right for me to assume your business
But maybe this notion you can entertain
In the spirit of this great party's blitheness
The thought of your father in hunger is plain
To contemplate is to save him from such Hell
Coin is not with me, but I've plans to attain
Repay all when I storm my old citadel

Journey with me, grace me with your company
Allow our life stories to run parallel
With you gone, food will stretch more abundantly
Your father will lose the extra mouth to feed
He need not worry about your gluttony
It's for him I stand with my heart full and plead
Join me, watch as I take back my rightful place
And return with riches to buy all you need."

The girl is struck silent as he makes his case
Our king, master of words, our great Lord-Supreme
Watch as her expression turns white as her lace
Her breath catches as she's offered her life's dream
Music from festivities near drowns her voice
As unending delight flows through her bloodstream
    "An offer, for sure," are her words of rejoice
    "It spins with rings of fact. I see the logic
    A proposal that makes my concerns devoice."

In her mind, our king's words are pathologic
They dance with other ideas, infecting
Replacing them with only the hypnotic
Persuasion of his modest plan perfecting
A nibble of her lip as his plan slithers
Wrinkled brow, alluring and unsuspecting
Then she speaks, looking away as she dithers
    "'Tis not my choice but my father we must ask
    Perhaps there is wisdom with him," she blithers

But then, as if summoned by God with a task
The old peasant comes and clasps his sweet daughter
    "My child, venture out so he may fill my cask
    With wine, ale, and endless amounts of water
    Food given by you, given by our great king
    Only then can we avoid my manslaughter
    Allow me to obtain my annual ring
    A boundless opportunity lies ahead
    The time has come to cut Wortstath's apron string
    Our great king, master of all, even the dead!
    Chosen by God to rule us lowly cretins
    And now he has chosen you, do as he's said
    Earn me good standing, assure that our house wins
    Then we shall feast like this party every night,"
Her father says, pulling her close as he grins
    "Your chance is here to escape this awful blight
    Be sure, let none of his wants waver or waste
    Stand ready, beautiful and proud to delight
    Ensure his fickle trust is never misplaced

Woe is to the woman that is not faithful
Lucky death for her, while family's disgraced
Let nothing you experience be baneful
You're on to the life you finally deserve
A life of discovery, my dear Angel."

Angel! The name our king pulls from mind's reserve
Not crucial but helpful in his quest to bed
This angel called Angel memory would serve
To be amused in his pursuit of bloodshed
Our great king clasps his fortune with both his hands
Fate is with him now, keeping his ego fed
Rightly so as he authors brilliant plans
Finally, now they're to come to fruition
With the Father cheering him on from the stands

Our king's and Krios' Heavenly audition
With one granted victory, kinship on high
And moronic Krios denied admission

The farmer watches, with red eyes, fate solidify
The strings' frayed ends fixed for an end that will satisfy

CHAPTER 4

The men of the Hand are stoic behemoths
Beneath their shrouds are faces of mystery
But the one certainty was their vehemence
Who would deny them, given their history?
To their Majesty, five men in reverence
Gazing at the head of their consistory
Now, charge in sight, they work for deliverance
A most arduous task, hardest of their lot
Minds steadied through reminders of temperance

Keep up, you great warriors and argonauts!
Beside you walks King Wrenfrey of Triastein
A fact that he'd rightly ne'er let be forgot
A king of kings from a bloodline of bloodlines
A drinker of the venom of scorpions
And whose sacred birth caused the stars to align

Deep breaths, you great warriors and champions!
Contain your fear and shelter your jealousy
And one day you can serve on his galleons

But for now escort him to your Majesty
Your tomorrow they discuss with imminence
Weigh your reality with their fantasy

March on, you great warriors and militants
But not too fast, it's not just their charge present
A shy maid among them, boundless innocence
Raising up the spirits of all malcontent
A guest of the king, naïve to say the least
All but blind to the ravenous man's intent

She left her old life to have a new one pieced—
Together by those she did not truly know
Surely to become nothing more than deceased
Struggling to keep up with life's new tempo
But she presses forward, winning their respect
Demonstrating her resolve was not just show

The group of seven journey through land suspect
Deeper and deeper into territory—
Never before seen by king or his subject
It is there they see it in all its glory

The home of the Hand, castle of their master
A stone monument, whispered purgatory
A treasure free of seer and forecaster
A gem where past and future share the present
Where you can't travel to through any pastor
The Hand brought the two forth, finally content

But their work was not done, more to ready for
They would carry it themselves without lament
For the Majesty they completely adore
Who claimed their spirits and gave them their purpose
Whose time has come and waits just beyond the door

Quiet around them as they leave the surface
Angel's full of inadequacy's punctures
The poor girl feels her presence a disservice
Her simple gaze is drawn to massive structures
Never before has she seen such awed splendour
The peasant hasn't witnessed other cultures
Following the Hand, she was a pretender
Her serf garb a stain upon the pedestal

But fear not, here he comes, her great defender
Frey knew she thought it was all incredible
Her slender arms wrap around her tiny frame
Learning majesty wasn't hypothetical

Servants line the walls to fill their master's aim
Pallor skin pieced together these entities
The harder he looked, the more grey they became
Like the Hand's men, shrouds hide their identities
Air of bitter chill but burning loyalty—
Has them never seeking out serenities
This way they demonstrate to their royalty
As long as both lives' rivers flow together
They'll mop every floor, stock every toiletry
They'll do what's asked 'till they're claimed by the nether

Their minds and hearts content, and their souls at rest
Promised freedom from torment's hateful tether

They wait amongst emptiness made manifest
Walls that climb to Heaven decorated bare
Halls stretched into blinding light left unexpressed
Leaves your eyes wandering with nowhere to stare
Yet staring is all Angel pet can muster
Words leading only to a silent prayer
Impressive to her despite its lacklustre
She could search and explore until she was lame
Frey knew to set right her obvious fluster

"Proper grandeur you'll not find here, it's quite tame."
Our king says to her, "It's true. I've seen finer
     The halls of my own keep would put these to shame
     Tapestries and rugs by the best designer
     Statues on fountains pooling crystal water
     Armour so polished they'd blind a diviner
     Vases by the most experienced potter
     But this resplendence must be overwhelming
     For a common provincial farmer's daughter."

Angel, cheered by the exchange he is helming
That she speaks her mind, understanding achieved
     "I fear becoming lost in such a dwelling
     Castles are much bigger than I first perceived
     Such abundance of chambers, side rooms, and halls
     Did your keep ever cause you to be deceived?"

Our king laughs as he leads them past bare stone walls
    "All the time!" our grand Wrenfrey answers in truth
    "The trick's not to let anyone hear your bawls
    And to catch a servant, keeping yourself couth
    'An urgent matter for you in the throne room
    Come, I will follow to ensure it is sooth
    Oh, it seems I'm mistaken, folly's in bloom'
    Then you leave, more mindful, but none the wiser
    Victoriously escaping your own tomb."

Angel laughs with her dubious advisor
Relieved to hear this man of men say such things
Threatening to burst from her like a geyser
That all minds are human, even a great king's
    "Is your own castle truly more ambitious?
    Here I understand where royal ego springs
    And see the holding of the avaricious
    What alterations could possibly be made
    To a place that already feels fictitious?"

Wrenfrey took her hand, happy to serenade
Placing the delicate creature on his arm
Keen to apply architectural first-aid
    "First some paintings, nothing to raise one's alarm
    Works of fascinating concepts but tasteful
    Candelabra to each to highlight their charm

    And second, all this empty space is wasteful
    Add displays of your armour and weaponry
    Something to show off the brutal and graceful

Third, to tie the place together, bestow me
Draped curtains of deepest royal violet
The colour of my house, gems from memory

But not to compare continent 'gainst islet
Not all can be as gifted or capable
One with charm, the other, say, inviolate

Last, for my final change, inescapable
Me on my throne before my gawking subjects
Reality so close it's unbreakable
Dressed to the nines with my personal effects
They'll shower me with the fruits of my labour
As their one true king stomps forth at his apex."

His words are fact, as natural as nature
Silenced only by slabs of obsidian
Colossal doors to the Majesty's chamber
A monstrous gate to a Hell of Stygian—
Nightmares laid throughout, the Hand our king's Charon
Slithering across are the ophidian
Covered in such blackness that swallows up dawn
They curl around a flower that never dies
That watches moments until all are foregone
Angel's grip on Frey tightens, tears in her eyes
Her self overcome by unnamed emotion
Darkness trying to dull her constant sunrise
King Wrenfrey understands her body's notion
That danger lies within, perhaps beyond God

But he would have revenge, his true devotion
He didn't work hard to have a door defraud—
Him of his courage. Pride, the instigator
Wounded, bruised, but he needn't remain a sod

Beyond was a promise of something greater
The power to take care of that Krios rat
Frey's to meet his fellow exterminator

So we come ever closer to the famed autocrat
Uncompromising, ruthless, and not one for chitchat

CHAPTER 5

Crossing the brink, the bargain is accepted
Warping 'round them, burning into their remains
Their roles are cast but are not as expected

And with as much subtlety as hurricanes
Our proud King Wrenfrey marches on without fear
He's ready to throw off his old serfdom's chains
Greatness enters this Majesty's subpar sphere
He knows we wish to meet so he hurries there
Now that our time is advancing ever near
Our marvellous king who is without compare
Preparing to meet his new alter ego
For a joyous moment he foresaw fanfare

But only absence of sound 'cross the plateau
To hear the drop of his footsteps on the floor
His shallow breathing gaining the room's echo

He stalks to a shape enthroned, sorrow's encore
Face hidden by shadows that sway and obscure
A mind of its own, the veil twists back and fore

A shroud like the subjects, but dark and impure
Like cold black fire, this demon magic dances
This demon dancing for lost souls to immure

Our king strays from God each step he advances
Trapped in the gaze of Lucifer, of Satan
He understands he has run out of chances
They'll take our king's immortal soul to straighten
The Hand's ruler, their Majesty, incarnate
With a heavy stare that lets only fate in
Used to control Hell's natives, to dominate
The weight aging our king's muscles and innards
Let's hatred, guilt, dread fester and copulate
The wake of its stare leaving behind blizzards
Freezing, chilling, biting of umbral abyss
Judgment starts in the limbs, works its way inwards
Knees weak, pants warm with the heat of your own piss
To your chest, compress ribs, tightening your lungs
Advancing to your mind, your head to dehisce

But then it's gone, freed by tranquillity's rungs
Warmth to chase the cold, stillness to calm the wind
Rose envelopes, protecting from devil tongues
Angel, his angel, makes the darkness rescind
Hand on his, her aura strong enough for two
As to not let his being be further sinned

Vitality returns to his breast anew
Eyes focus on the Majesty, but play tricks?
For not Lucifer, but a human in view

Face veiled from sight, yet new reason to transfix
Not a lord of honour or a brute of strength
It's a woman that rules this River of Styx
Our king's optimism once again at arm's length
As an eternity passes through the space
Building intensity to a degree's nth
Both titans wait for the other to lose face
By giving silence a scare and speaking first

But it's the Hand who breaks the stubborn showcase
Gazing at their head with unquenchable thirst
Gone for so long, too long, but finally home
The leader steps forth and speaks, his words well-versed
    "We return from the land of cheatgrass and loam
    Your bidding we've done, ready to do once more
    To serve as the ultimate design's prodrome
    A never-ending mission, our souls we swore
    From you our strength, your ideals we enshrine
    For they are ours, and each of us with a score
    Let us show our zeal as goals again align
    Escorted from across into our between
    Here is the man Wrenfrey, King of Triastein."

Silence and chill once more dominate the scene
Stillness, this mysterious benefactor
A statue from which no emotion could gleam

But stone, gadder, lawful or malefactor
Wrenfrey would seize all in his quest of judgment
There's not a single step he wouldn't factor

Krios' prize for his selection of lodgment
Wrenfrey will take back his crown, torn from his skull
The stench of his foe's defeat will be pungent

But first there were words from the queen he must cull
This brimstone fiend was his royal salvation
He'd make sure she did not write him off as null
    "Queen," he says, replacing pride with placation
    "Your servant speaks true, King Wrenfrey, in the flesh
    I come to compliment your keen mentation
    Keeping good sense during the world's endless thresh
    Despite your humble womanly appearance
    You've the mind of a man, rare in one so fresh
    Smart to rise above your peers' disappearance

    When asked for command of their armies, they laughed
    Rights of brotherhood were lack of adherence
    Turned away, left me to my sinking life raft
    Thanks is given and thanks is to be received
    When I raise your standing above those too daft
    From those whose dignity and virtue were cleaved
    Unite our kingdoms, your command, our command
    Show our enemy our rage must be believed—"

The Majesty on high holds up her pale hand
Cutting off our king's oleaginous rant
Not wanting his ego to further expand
The room loses its echo of sycophant
And muteness prevails over the two once more
As he waits for the great army she would grant

Uncross and cross her legs, she contemplates war
Her ice gaze burning through her shroud's layered silk
It scorches the proud man who justice calls for
It finds the one at his side, not of his ilk
Crimson hair, ashen eyes, plain dress, lacking airs
Malnutrition stunted height with skin like milk
Clueless for when life would catch her unawares
Soft and quiet, familiar reflection found
Let us see if there's anything left upstairs
The Majesty moves, her audience spellbound
Her loyal friends bracing for her coming song
Where loss, affliction, and agony resound

    "A king." Shadows douse torches, stripping the strong
    "Before me." Voice of pain turns air acidic
    "I see not." Blood drips from ears from torture's throng

Breath of fire and smoke, still a demon's mimic
Pull tears at the corner of our good king's eyes
Makes him wish his poor mind was syphilitic
Insanity the only way one survives
Twisting metal with your teeth, cutting your gums
He's marked, never to be clean again, he cries

But again his light in the dark, Angel comes
    "Fear not these words, my lord, it's a cock's display
    To puff their feathered chest and peck at your crumbs
    Put it from your thoughts. You're not some common stray
    After all, was she not the one to call you?
    With offers of your sworn enemy as prey?"

Our king, generous with his time, listens through
Her encouragement needed against this foe
But he smiles, pretending he already knew
Bad to let them think, lest more they think they know
Woman or peasant, and double if they're both
He straightens up, keeping her on his elbow
A small step forward, he turns back to Hell's growth
    "Your words ring true, dear queen, no king at this time
    Stolen my livelihood and my brothers' oath
    To protect from those that harm and evil's slime
    Contorted by Krios, seduced by his word
    No God to clear them of this most heinous crime
    I come to you, hopeful rumours were unheard
    Hopeful for my last chance of reclamation
    Hopeful that your loyalties have not been spurred."

The queen answers back, the head of her nation
Once more in that voice to cleave Heaven from thought
And yearn for a sparing pre-death cremation
    "These rumours I've experienced, know what's wrought
    You say he is our enemy, fallen king
    Yet he's come to us, laughed with me and my lot
    I've seen him fight for my honour, feel pain's sting
    In times of need, he cradled me to his chest
    Tears on his face, his emotions in full-swing."

    "Forgive me, dear queen," our king speaks from his breast
    "That man's no more than a ploy wrapped in a scheme
    He wishes for your throne, this I can attest
    He blinds you with fake adoring, let's you dream

Behind closed doors, he turns those loyal against
He sees you without husband and with regime
He knows omniscient justice will be dispensed
When blind Justice removes the veils from my friends
And she allows his trial to be commenced
He needs protection from his ill-gotten ends
And he'll use you to legitimize his claim

It's this, before his integrity has bends
Brothers in all but blood. We both felt the same
Promised to share what we had with the other
Countless vows and pledges, his true claim to fame
All of it matters not to this blood brother

You wake to attack, your wife and baby scared
A fire set to engulf you, smoke to smother
You flee only to watch your worst fears be bared
Krios from the dark, slits the throat of your love
There is no sickness to which it is compared
A more horrid action one couldn't speak of
It'll be the same for you once he gets his way
Ring on your finger and guillotine above
Allow me to protect you from his vile sway
Together we can stop his reign of terror
Only then can we end this endless doomsday."

The queen weighs the words of this bad news bearer
Her voice on her bloodless lips, ready to fly
Storming all with thoughts their lives are in error

"Krios killed your wife?"

Our king pressing through his ears' desire to die
Nodded, solemn. "Indeed, he wielded the blade
    Love and son. This you can expect as ally:
    Smiles and delights, parties and promises made

    Broken upon the burnt ruin of your house
    Left to wander with only your features staid
    So let it be I you select to espouse
    On this beautiful day of alliances
    Before Krios' devils of betrayal rouse."

Shadows whip as she speaks, the room silences
    "Justice reigns over all, in this life and next
    Despite what some may hold in their biases
    Immune does not exist, from prey to apex

    I take on the charge of fallen King Wrenfrey
    And find compensation for those who were vexed
    This will be my absolution, this the way
    Let he who lies be victim to women's wrath
    That with rectitude, there is no room for grey."

King Wrenfrey is gleeful, life a primrose path
Listening to his future take proper shape
Naught scarier than women bent on bloodbath

The queen goes on with her auditory rape
    "This fallen king will show us his character

He will demonstrate that it did not escape
During his time with hunter and forager
Still the man that resided in his castle
Prove he's still his legacy's inheritor
He is to perform three tasks as my vassal
Each imperative to the coming onslaught
He's sure to complete all, adroit and facile."

Perform? The Hand didn't note this small caveat
Like some jester? Our king was taken aback
To play the fool in this unrelenting plot?
Was his pride in need of another attack?
And not just one task, but three to grind him down
The writer of our king's story is a hack

But again his angel softens his deep frown
    "My lord, I see on your face condemnation
    Don't feel pressed to embarrassment for your crown
    Fixing a wrong should act as your fixation
    Just a few hiccups until all is righted
    That's all that this is, then only elation
    Stay calm and don't let yourself be benighted
    Reminiscence will lead to mind's clarity."
She speaks softly, the queen makes her affrighted

But again her words gain popularity
So our glorious king gives a gracious bow
Towards the queen, his speech to his parity
    "My attention to your tasks, I give my vow

None will break my focus, none will ruin me
Or let our Heavenly Father smite me now."

Our king is one step closer to her army
Years he's waited. What is a couple months more?
'Haps he'll win more than men from this Majesty

The queen presses on. There's much to answer for
She proceeds back to her earlier business
Her throat relinquishes the sound all deplore
    "Before he receives his just prize, we witness
    He must prove himself with three distinct trials
    Manifest for us his cerebral fitness
    To use sword or speech, his aggression or wiles
    My friends, we need him to do what must be done
    My Hand will chaperon to observe his guiles
    Each trial further cements our decision

    Listen well, fallen king, for I won't repeat
    Treasures with my house seal to heal your scission
    Held by three others. The first you are to meet
    Resting in a woods cabin, known as the Witch
    Harassed by townsfolk, her goodwill's now deplete
    Her and her Sons' souls said to be black as pitch
    Said to kidnap children to serve their dark lord
    And corpses of trespassers thrown in the ditch
    It's there you must hurry to claim your reward
    She withholds the first chest inside her cabin
    Fallen king, you'll not let yourself be ignored

You will listen not to her Devil's Latin
You will enter her shelter to take what's yours
On your own accomplishment, you will fatten
But should you go astray, return on all fours
Beg my forgiveness, implore my acceptance
Let the mortification seep from your pores

Plead your sin before us all, show us your repentance
And we will listen and debate our acquiescence."

CHAPTER 6

There our exquisite king goes, cape aflutter
The grim shadows not diminishing his shine
Choice muscles and rich mind, our bread and butter
Our mouths water with mere thoughts of his jawline
Our dear young Angel pet understands our plight
Long she's watched him, staring forlorn for some sign

Such a regal man, she thought, such a sad sight
His wistful expression she tried to break through
Yet she's brushed off with reasons that held no bite
Her peasantry, her womanity, her view
His mystery unraveled before the queen
The curious Angel realized what's true

His plea allowed her a peek behind the screen
Family murdered by one they saw as friend
Neither would she speak of something so unclean
Her soft heart bleeds as she tries to comprehend
Loved ones are lost. This she sadly knew too well
But a Judas kiss? A horror story penned
She'd do her best to keep him from heartbreak's spell

She'd steel herself, be a shield for our great king
But we'll see ourselves how much dark she can quell

This journey may be this girl's last depending—
On how you view the end of this haunting tale
But we speak too soon, let the next inkling sing

   "Flower," the Hand leader's voice slips out his veil
Watchful as he comes to walk beside Angel
     "Tell me your thoughts. Meeting my queen can assail
     Upon my first encounter, it was painful
     Though now I hear nothing but amends inside
     Hope swells you're not scared by something thought baneful?
     If needed, I will stand by you to provide—
     A strong presence or quiet conversation
     I promise not to heckle or to deride."

Relief fills her across this unknown nation
Titan, Angel pet refers to him as such
He greeted her without exasperation
A gentle giant with a chivalrous touch
His wife must have several lucky rabbits' feet
Ah, to have such a prize, one wishes too much

   "I found her sad, though true her voice was no treat,"
Angel's words float on the forest's carefree breeze
     "But to have many love you is no mean feat
     I heard what you said. She made you all at ease
     I could feel your devotion down to the bone
     Her presence alone made you want to appease

Yet woe I felt as her presence *is* alone
Someone special is supposed to be with her
But they're gone... ah, I speak of what is unknown

Tell me of your true love, your wife I refer
A woman beyond compare, I have no doubt
What type of woman does a giant prefer?
One grounded, hale in heart, and with stature stout?
Perhaps soft, delicate, but a razor's wit?
Maybe strong as he, to handle any bout?"

Yet she witnesses a saddening spirit
Titan, though his expression veiled from her view
A wash of emotion one can't counterfeit
Angel's voice comes, "I speak without thought to you
    She must have been incredible to evoke—
    Such sorrow with her passing, both loves so true."

But Titan stops her, shakes his head, voice awoke
    "Fear not, flower, she has not passed. My wife lives
    My heart breaks for it's been long since last we spoke
    And our last conversation where anger gives—
    Falseness to words out of worry and concern
    Things were said my soul only hopes she forgives."

Angel speaks now, "And why do you not return?
    No doubt she has these same feelings in her breast
    Such grief now means this is not a love to spurn
    After, you should go to her, have all addressed

Talking will remedy more than avoidance
And you can both put your misery to rest."

Titan lets loose a sigh. "Had I clairvoyance…
    Duty keeps me, and should she herself find me
    The tears I'd weep would act as my soul's voidance
    Not as simple as making a heartfelt plea
    Now let us part ways 'fore your eavesdropping king—
    Has his neck snap from his craning head's degree."

There's a cough from Wrenfrey as he feels the sting—
Of being caught, cheeks flood red, eyes dart away
Leading to Angel's laughter, musical thing
She goes to our king to fall under his sway
Walking together, a wolf beside a fawn
They hurry on to meet the end of the day
Where their travelling becomes a camp, tents drawn
A crisp nip in this forest of blackened leaves
With her warm blankets, she plans her liaison

Such a bizarre time, her amongst swords and greaves
She is a farmer's daughter, of quiet folk
Now she runs with men, to be apparent thieves
But she's made an oath, one she wouldn't revoke
Angel looks to Frey, sureness fills her chilled form
Purpose on his brow, he gives the fire a poke

Her eyes stir the hairs on his neck, he smiles warm
A smile just for her as he holds out his hand

Beckoning gently, he's eager to perform
    "Shaking like a leaf, home amongst this woodland
    But a woman shaking for any reason
    It's against my aristocratic command."
His sharp gaze finds hers, sultry for the season
It scorches her skin, her cheeks turn ruby red
    "Unless, of course, she shakes like men of treason
    Due to countless bouts of love upon my bed."
The tension is thick, the flames eating the air
Then he grins, cheeky and childlike, his joke said
    "But in truth, come sit by the fire, I can share
    The warriors of the Hand are not in need
    They choose the cold of night, the moon's silver stare
    While I watch the crimson flames force it to cede
    Humanity's primeval dancing partner
    As liable to help you as make you bleed."

His stares become long, guile lost to this charmer
Thoughts whisked here, there, and then away to nowhere

But he's brought back before getting much farther
Hand on his, crimson flame against crimson hair
Angel catches him, giving strength to our king
    "To hear your grim tale was more than I could bear
    And to hear in such a way was a cruel thing
    Wounds opened, shouted before all who could hear
    Tragedy told to those who don't feel its sting
    Wish I could be your sorrowful river's weir
    Diverting your memories of misfortune

But all I can truly do is to be here
To joust with you like a soldier of fortune
To help you gather these keys to your kingdom
And to ensure everyone gets their portion
You are not alone, Frey, as king or pilgrim
My hope you do not forget but can move on
With aid from all who gather with their wisdom."

Our king is silent, stunned as a newborn fawn
A discomfort builds in his chest. It's too much...
In Angel's face, Wrenfrey sees she who is gone
The terror building, destruction is nonesuch
With the fire raging, she raises her hand up
The glint of blade travelling… no, it's too much!
She is standing there, wanting a soul to sup
A knife at her back but delicate in frills
Agaricus but secretly a death cup

War wages in his mind, between two mad wills
Angel observes this unusual display
His head full with more than what mere sadness fills
Perhaps she did understand his mind's decay
Why was she here and not with her old father?
How could she have left him, fallen so astray?
She should have rejected our good king's proffer
She was naught but a fool, stuck in a forest
With all matter of murderer and robber

Wind whips intensifying as dread's chorist
The base howls of memories from her future

Here comes the end for this flower effloresced
Her blood is draining, the wound needs a suture
She's shaken, mentally and literally

Round eyes, scratched cheek, a young Boy breaks her stupor
His toothy grin frees her from Death's litany
With a grin, the Boy speaks, "It's the Witch's magic,
    Here in her wood she spreads hate liberally
    A crotchety old crone who makes lives tragic
    She ate abandoned babes, each time her curse grew
    It's true! It is! She's the Devil's choragic!"

Frey rouses with Angel to meet their guru
Our king speaks: "You mean 'the Devil's choragus'
    Don't fret, a stranger corrected me once too
    And your witches theory is not mere foreguess
    To affect my mind, find myself overcome
    She must be strong, this daughter of Erebus
    Won't be swayed, even if made blind, deaf, and dumb
    Though it appears sentiments not wholly shared
    Look now, my Angel, the Hand has left us mum."

Her ashen eyes gaze, but their campsite is bared
The Hand is gone, darkness has swallowed them whole

Wait, hold, in the trees! With the shadows they've paired
The shrouds are watching, observing our king's soul
Angel pet reaches for them but they recede
Like ghosts they haunt, still under their queen's control

Shivers trace paths up her spine and spread their seed
The ways of royalty are much too undue
Perhaps toxins in gold made reason impede

She turns back toward the little Boy in blue
Dressed in Byzantine splendour with his surcoat
No expense is spared for this male ingenue
She kneels to head height, like a mother to dote
 "My, where did you come from? In the woods alone?
 You could get hurt, danger is always afloat
 Stay with us tonight, so you're not on your own
 In the morn we can bring you to your keeper
 Pray, what is the name attached to these cute bones?"

Angel taps his button nose, falling deeper
He giggles, a red blush coming to his face
Neither knowing the other was the Reaper

 "Ask less about him and more about this place,"
Our duty bound king breaks in, him commanding
 "Boy, you know of the Witch, your footsteps retrace—
 With us in tow. She has something outstanding
 That which is mine to claim, a component box."

The Boy nods, eyes alight with understanding
 "I know of what you speak, handled by that pox
 I can help you with that evil hag, a treat
 Watch me, chiefly you, my lady, I'm who stalks
 I'm a man from families of the elite

Let us go right now and catch her by surprise
I'll slay the Witch and place her head at your feet!"

Angel chuckles at this hero on the rise
One too many fantastic tales at bedtime
It brings her back, before plagues did brutalize—
Her village of Wortstath and the death toll's climb
Blamed for them Angel was, her father broken
A scary point in her life, less than sublime
A tug on her hand, the brave Boy has spoken

She speaks, "We should wait until the sun is high
We can talk when everyone has awoken
The Witch is misunderstood, I'm sure that's why—
She's thought of as evil and persecuted."

Our king gives a sympathetic smile and sigh
The Boy mirroring him, his face transmuted
Comfort in the form of a hand on her cheek

Wrenfrey speaks, his knowledge on this well-suited
"Your beauty shines when you give voice to the meek
However, this cruel Witch is anything but

We must heed the queen's words to find what we seek
An eater of children, the Bible she's smut
The Boy knows the legend, of her Devil's breed
No doubt his people also know she's clear-cut
Could so many be wrong? You have to concede

The queen, a good judge of character, swears it
And with such a head on her rumours don't feed
Do you believe she would make our journey writ—
If she didn't possess all intelligence?
Tear not, we'll be done before the Earth's sunlit."

Angel hears his words, unsure if arrogance—
Causes Wrenfrey to speak with such conviction
Or if it's really using one's common sense
She's not seen magic, dealt with its affliction
Sheltered by her father, away from the world
Perhaps the royals could sort truth from fiction
Blessed by God, from their mouths His Word is unfurled

She acquiesces to their experience
Angel says, "Before accusations are hurled
    Let's be good-natured but still keep our good sense
    After all, if she knows magic and curses
    Would it not be grave to make her skills dispense?"

The Boy is thoughtful, nodding with her verses
Our king joins in as well, "Superb idea
    Fake our purpose, so her evil disperses."

The Boy's eyes widen. He says, "That Medea
    Witch and kid killer, she won't suspect a thing
    Catch her by surprise, we'll be her Hosea."

She lifts her hand to correct the Boy and king
Deception and a prophet of doom, not quite—
What this angel called Angel had been thinking

But the two were already into the night
Leaving her to catch up, her lips loose a sigh
A glance to the woods hurries her to their sight

Titan watches as the first moment of truth grows nigh
Observers for their queen who they can never deny

CHAPTER 7

Water flows slowly across the riverbed
The merry whistle of singing birds quiet
Reminders of where innocence once dared tread
This forest boasting a familiar diet
Observers vigilant as incomers move
Some hope for oblivion, wish to try it

Others are ready, waiting to carve their groove
The beasts of this dark place, this plot their domain
Anticipating their next moment to prove
Their hunt under the moon, their claws and fangs strain
They yearn to grab hold of the meat before them
Sink into flesh in hopes blood cools burning pain

Only the Hand contains their eager mayhem
Superior protectors, chosen shrewdly
Superior predators, Majesty's gem
Hypocrites those outside might call them rudely
As they deny the chase and pursuit of prey
While lurking behind trees like stalkers lewdly

Words brought on by uninformed thoughts that betray
Lack of understanding, a willing blindfold
Of all the roles those in this small world must play
Knights on a chessboard chasing the pawns they're told
As the queen waits, 'til all turns superfluous
Watching their marks to see what events unfold

"It's culture and sophistication for us,"
Frey speaks, making conversation with the Boy
His minute double listens as he speaks thus:
 "Let none tell you different. The world is your toy
 We are of a divergent, more refined stock
 Some may disagree; it's nothing but a ploy
 An idea to poison you like hemlock
 Ne'er turn back lest the knives of those 'concerned' reach
 Our shadows, where jealousy and deceit stalk
 They care not for the downtrodden as they preach
 They want your power, think your riches are theirs
 Parasites wishing for a fool they can leech."

The Boy takes in our great king's lessons and cares
Lessons our fragile Angel finds worrying
An impressionable Boy to hear such scares
Too soon to his adulthood, he's hurrying
Our king speaks as though all are potential foes
A future of loneliness he's currying
Knowing him, she's aware how those thoughts arose
Perhaps she'll talk to the Boy in privacy
Say backstabbery is not all the world knows
That it's not always about your primacy

But for now she'd dare not embarrass our king
To steal his audience would be piracy
How he must enjoy the Boy under his wing
Lost experiences wanting to be claimed
Robbed of his poor son, but with knowledge wellspring

O' let his enthusiasm be untamed
What's a small conversation between two men?

    "There, look!" the Boy says. "The hut of the Witch famed
    Swallowing itself into the swampy glen
    Corruption pulses from it, killing the trees
    Look there, blood pools under a sacrificed hen
    The bushes and flowers tremor to appease—
    Their Daughter of Lilith, their evil mistress
    She drinks in their fear, their life force hers to seize
    Just the sight of her home causes all duress
    Where she eats kids to make her spells the strongest
    She steals away my prayers, this heathenness
    It's why I forget them at bedtime, honest!
    And why I sometimes spit at my family."
The Boy shakes his head as if in a contest—
Of chagrin. "It is a true calamity
    For a young boy's mind to be made illicit
    Who knows what else she'll make me do? Alchemy?
    Leave chores undone or steal an extra biscuit?
    Such injustice in this world, such injustice
    To be in the hands of one so sadistic."

So serious his face, commitment lustrous
It makes Angel scoop him into her pale arms
A chuckle from her as he kicks up a fuss
    "How cute you are," she says to his boyish charms
    "Dressed to the nines, but still there's a child inside
    Whimsy's the same, whether in manors or farms
    Come here now, let your crocodile tears be dried."

The Boy pulls free of his giggling prison
With a huff, he straightens his coat with hurt pride
He keeps himself calm, his voice hasn't risen
    "You dare think I'm some drudge in another skin?
    My father is above the poor/rich schism
    He sits upon a throne, practically God's twin
    And you call me a child? I'm ten summers old
    Can you even count to ten, you mewling quim?"

Frey laughs. "You remind me of me, truth be told
    But you must learn tact when with the fairer sex
    To earn one's affection is the greatest gold
    To have them at your side, proving your apex
    Delicate to accentuate your manhood
    A clear testament to make your rivals vex
    If you wish to be a real man, as you should
    A woman makes your accomplishments tenfold
    Now, Boy, nod your head to show you've understood."

The Boy nods as he listens, already sold
He's absorbing all our grand king has to teach
A quill-less chronicler, etched to mind all told

Our king refocused his attention and speech:
    "Listen well to my plan. Angel, you're the spark
    To the cruel Witch's hut you will go to beseech
    As a beggar, call on her gifts of the dark
    Ask to enter the home, it's unsafe outside
    Look for ophidian and flower, our mark
    While her back is turned, pretend still, your eyes wide
    But snatch our first prize and move to the window
    I'll grab it and we can leave this countryside."

The Boy is in awe, but Angel pet less so
To wander by herself to the Witch's homestead
One known for eating children and bringing woe
A shiver in her spine as cold as the dead

But our all-knowing king senses her dismay
He generously gives strength, negating dread
    "Be pleased, my Angel, for it's your words at play
    You're free to speak with the Witch, to seek the truth
    And with all alive at the end of the day
    She'll be less concerned with one still holding youth
    You're the best for this, least suspicious by far
    But your nerves are on fire, mine as well, forsooth!

    We can do this together, our skills on par
    Centre yourself. Think of the rewards to come
    To do this would help heal my old life's deep scar
    And bring you closer to your father's filled drum

You have it in you, power you fear to grab
I see it. Now's time to use it, not succumb."

Fair Angel pet entranced by his gift of gab
Gulps down all her doubts, feels her terror subside
Chest now heaves with thoughts of pulling off this scab
Her quiver of anticipation implied
As her eyes dart, eager to do our lord's work
Dear strong Angel feels his great plan must be tried
The Boy watches as she's sent out, them to lurk
Agonizingly slow steps, she plays her part
The scared serf journeying to the profane kirk
So convincing, it's a role she knows by heart

The whispers of lost souls, the call of the crows
Brought to this darkened place by the Witch's dark art
Stumbling in her walk, jumping at shadows
The front door coming both too slow and too fast
A look behind shows naught but forest echoes
With our king out of her sight, she could not last
What was she to do without him to lean on?

Lo! She sees a shape in the woods, her fear cast!
Her terror given form as Lucifer's spawn?
Unmoving, yet it presses on Angel pet
With a sadness and pain, a heartbreak ne'er gone

But its stalking spotted, hiding place beset
It's gone quick as it came. Angel's gaze the cause
Perhaps imagination conjured a threat?

Angel steels herself in this land lacking laws
Pressing on, with the crack of a thunderstorm
Yet with no rain, it felt like Satan's applause

Not a drop fell upon her trembling form
No blaze of lightning flashed in the darkened sky
But she feels its pinpricks like an insect swarm
Can hear their buzzing as the lost children's cry
They bite and tear at her regained confidence
Pincers ripping her skin, in hunger they vie

The thunder comes harder, growing more intense
Within her chest the thunder threatens to burst
To this Witch's magic, there is not one defence
She can't do it! Can't! She doesn't want to be cursed!
She's at the door now, her hand freezes mid-knock
Her knees no longer hold up, her strength dispersed
To dirt she falls unable to rid this pock
Teeth chatter, mind whirls, as now she is the prey
Despair threatens to take her; she hears the lock

The clunk and squeal of the door as it's lifted away
Out pokes a small head and a voice asks: "Are you okay?"

CHAPTER 8

Appearances deceive, trick to fool the eyes
Simple for a witch, this manifestation
A tiny girl is certainly no surprise
Ivory hair, pale rose eyes, cursed creation
Like spider silk, her hair catches in the breeze
Brushing sickly white skin, pure enervation
Blood eyes stare down at Angel pet on her knees
Large and round, they're plopped in a thin sunken face
No malice, no hatred, completely at ease
No… there is concern, Angel pet spies its trace
In this pallid young girl of maybe eight years
But hard to tell her age with sickness in place

She is peeking around the door and its gears
Opening her mouth to speak once more, she's caught—
In a coughing fit, Angel's head at last clears
To her feet, then scoop up the child. She feels hot
Without fear Angel pet enters the Witch's lair
Passing skulls, feathers, ingredients, witchknot

Dried blood dots the table, fetishes laid bare
A bed to the side, basin in the corner
Is this Angel really to help Satan's heir?

From the basin a washcloth to adorn her
Cool with water to bring down the girl's fever
The cherub relies on this new foreigner
Angel touches her pale cheek, not to leave her
As delicate as moth wings, body stick thin
How could one so small be the Great Deceiver?
And how did she come to this hovel's within?
The Boy spoke of there being children captive
Held hostage to be eaten, in this cabin

Angel's thoughts are silenced, our king is active
Suddenly pressing through the door with the Boy
Our illustrious king, ever adaptive
Moves with a purpose, unlike the hoi polloi
His alien royal presence shakes the hut
Here to collect like a taxman does octroi

"What luck we have," Wrenfrey says, his pride uncut
"No Witch to be seen, 'lest that near corpse be her
This place, stirring lesser men's food from their gut
The dizzying scent of blood mixing with myrrh
A more wretched hive of scum and villainy—
I doubt exists. A playground for Lucifer."

Our wise king spits with self-righteous bigotry
While the Boy ventures to Angel and her ward

He grabs the cherub's hand, smitten instantly
Distracted by beauty, much like her own lord
   "Never I've seen a girl made of snow and glass
   Look now! Her eyes open! Rose-red is what's stored
   One of the evils the Witch summoned en masse?
   Or one of the kids taken, their life force drained?
   Have no fear, no more shall danger come to pass!"

He speaks to her directly, purpose ordained
While Angel is called away by King Wrenfrey
Under his protective gaze, her fear constrained
He greets her warmly, a smile to rival day
Upon her grimy hand, he places a kiss
Uncaring of the dirt or smell of decay—
That covers her palm, sensing nothing amiss
He speaks, the rumble of his lips 'cross her skin
   "Amazing to endure a trial such as this
   You have the gratitude of this old has-been
   A lovely spectacle to see one so brave
   To freely enter this horrid house of sin

   Now let us search it or ask the foul Witch's slave
   Where lies our prize sealed with the flower and snakes
   So we may escape my poor man's nameless grave."

"Snakes and flower…" words form in a small voice's shakes

From the bed, held by the Boy, feverish face
The poor girl, she should be playing ducks and drakes
Instead, her eyes are glazed as her health gives chase

"In the cabinet... the top shelf I can't reach
Never to look, she said, 'lest my heart lose pace
Formed from all manner of trees, oak, spruce, and beech
For she who's out of time… she knows it's all up…"
The girl's eyes close, asleep, done with her odd speech

The Boy pats her hand. "Rage overflows my cup
Her soul is half-eaten, drained with her colour
With my righteous fury I will not letup
I know without her my life will be duller
This day I pledge to protect and to provide
All will be done. All we'll have is each other."

Frey leans to Angel, whisper in an aside
"Quite the thespian, he, wouldn't you agree?
Hm? Why do you laugh? And have your smile so wide?
Did I say something to make your sides split free?"

His confusion makes Angel laugh all the more
She touches his bearded cheek, delicate she
"Reminded of one, dramatic to his core,"
She says to our great king of humility
"Sweet, wise, and who acts as his own troubadour."

Outwards our king maintains his gentility
But he wonders at this mystery rival
Take care to maintain her arability
He says, "Let's move, we know not the arrival—
Of the Witch and her flock, with them the evil
Grab our prize 'fore we bet on our survival

Inside the cabinet, there for retrieval
Complete the Majesty queen's first inane task
To acquire what's mine by birthright primeval."

And it's there, as the girl said, no need to ask
A box of a size to contain jewellery
But with a smell no perfume could hope to mask
Snakes and flower writhe, almost illusory
Upon the wooden box's lid, twisting under
Shut tight, but this was no time for foolery
Our king can do nothing but look and wonder
Curiosity has our king in its throes
Curious to see what's inside to plunder

His eyes land on the girl with the gaze of rose
The Boy pushed aside as our king takes her hand
    "Little one who's seen the Witch, survived her woes
    More accustomed than us who're not of this land
    Seeped in her magic, into your blood and bone
    A favour, I must ask. Compliance is grand
    Open this box for us to see what's unknown
    A want in your own mind to see what's inside
    Lift the lid and we'll have ignorance dethrone."

Words are on Angel's lips, to condemn and chide
But a sudden feeling of need fills her breast
To see, like the face of a loved one who died
Closure ne'er to come, an unpassable test
Left to wander the lonely Earth as a ghost
Knowing life to be nothing but a cruel jest

This pet, she should be the one to see foremost
And so she let the sickly child lift the top
Trapped by her mystery need, the unsought host

Immediately all are assailed by slop
The smell of raw flesh and the sound of thumping
Inside entrails, organs, a heart that won't stop
Nerveless, yet they wriggle; bloodless, yet pumping
But not those of someone grown, heart walnut size
Perhaps... chicken, no sense conclusion jumping

But they know, all do, despite desperate lies
In this witch house, the eater of children's flesh
That babes aren't exempt from the Lord of the Flies

The girl closes the lid, horror ever fresh
Without a word, she lifts the box to our king
Understanding now her role in this cursed crèche
Wrenfrey with the box, sanity on a string
What could possibly be the meaning of this?
This is what the queen needs? Such a putrid thing!
Dark magic at work, he should not be remiss
But with vile Krios he must fight fire with fire
Soon all will be memory to reminisce

  "Out of the bed, girl, lest you're to join the pyre,"
Our king says, stalking to the hearth with intent
    "Boy, come take heed. We attend to something dire
    Take this torch so we may cleanse evil's torment
    Have no more lost to this wicked demon whore

Now! Hurry up! While my anger is still pent
Angel, grab the girl and get out, out the door
We ensure none of this tragedy survives
Burn it all down, every foul weed, leaf, and spore
Leave her nothing as we destroy her archives
Small victory for her many casualties
With knowledge she'll merely set up her new hives
At least, for a time, she won't trap more with ease
The queen is in luck that, for her, I've such need
Already I wonder at her mind's disease
To peddle with darkness, is it right or greed?
I care not to know, just that it's pure evil
And so we put an end to Lucifer's seed."

Outside, they stand to commit their upheaval
The Boy and our king standing tall with the torch
Flames licking the night for some souls' retrieval

The girl, with Angel, sees them approach the porch
She pushes away, runs to the king and Boy
Her laboured breaths like fire, her ailing lungs scorch
Like a wisp, looks and strength, lacking any joy
    "Please stop! She is not bad. You misunderstand,"
She pulls at our king's sleeve. She's tears to employ
    "She saved me when I was cast out of my land
    Her Sons found me, the three treat me as their own
    Care not about my red eyes, hair of white strand
    Proclaimed a plague bearer and a demon's drone
    I was always unwelcome 'til I found them
    I plead with you now. Please don't burn down my home."

The Boy, torch held, looks to our lord of mayhem
Our lord says, "You say she's good. And what we saw?
    A box of foul parts is enough to condemn!
    Or did you miss the offal? Your mind withdraw?
    Explain the children devoured by your saviour
    Their legacy as bones for the wolves to gnaw."

The white-haired girl is in tears, losing favour
    "Maybe they were sick like me. She can't save all
    Please, none were eaten!" Sick, her voice does quaver

On our great king's deaf ears are where her words fall
A hand on her shoulder. He says, "Don't you see?
    Had we not come, you would be the next she'd maul
    There is no wish in my heart to crush your glee
    But a witch is danger, fraught with exposure—
    To things too cruel for one so young and carefree
    Believe me in this and keep your composure
    You'll thank me once you're grown and mind is mature
    Glad that this dark part of your life has closure
    Angel, care for her as we cleanse the impure
    Begin now, Boy, let us free any trapped souls
    Our rightful place in Heaven this will secure."

Angel holds her close, no fight as the fire rolls
Consuming the dry wood, lighting up the sky
Night turning to day, chaos with no controls
Hiss of history going up in smoke nigh
Inside countless hours spent, memories made
And all that's left now is the girl's silent cry

"My fault," she says. "I let you in, let you raid
Where will I go? Or am I cursed once again?
I've betrayed her trust and the price must be paid."

Angel twists her 'round, corrections she would pen
At her level, face-to-face, she says, "Hear me,
You are blameless, a victim of where and when
All crossroads led here, perhaps its Fate's decree
But you're not the reason for this destruction
There is no need for you to say you're sorry."

Red eyes pierce her, blow past every obstruction
Grasp Angel's core, fill her veins with freezing ice
The swirling crimson, drowning out the ruction
Deed older than time inside, eclipsing vice
Blood meets blood as a flower's petals return
Another copy sprouts, it's a perfect splice
There is no difference that any can discern
Of this flower, there's only ever been one
One to care for, one to live for, one to spurn
Confusion mixed with heartbreak, a story spun
Raging, pleading, planning, reckoning, no peace
Unable to stop until her work is done

Then Angel's yanked free, pulled from drowning release
Her breaths coming hard, all she can see is red
The red of those eyes and our king's masterpiece
Its ashes catching in the wind, evil shed

With the coming of morning's brilliant light
The land is healed with the loss of that homestead

    "My Angel," Frey says to her. "We've won our fight
    And secured our first requirement, that damned box
    Though what that Majesty wants with such a sight
    I'm quite afraid to ask lest she end our talks
    Or perhaps I'd join her twisted collection
    Either way, her methods are unorthodox."

A chuckle puts an end to slight objection
The Boy comes and grabs the girl's arm. "My lady,
    It causes me pain to see your dejection
    Please listen to my request, nothing shady
    In a land not far, ruled by my great father
    Two nobles wish day and night for a baby
    Of impeccable beauty, their own daughter
    One to dress and care for, to love endlessly
    Now that I've freed you from this vile backwater
    You're perfect, your life improved tremendously

    Come with me and I'll ensure you're treated well
    I'll protect you, ne'er to worry helplessly
    With me by your side, you can journey through Hell
    Not a scratch will mar your snow white perfection
    For you, I'd even silence the Reaper's knell."

The girl nods, hiding her eyes from reflection
    "I will come with you, join this new family
    And hope I can once again find affection."

He's blind to her internal calamity
He's elated and with a grab of her wrist
They wander off to the forest happily

The left behind watch them go, cross off their list
Our succulent king admires Angel's beauty
Her flushed cheeks fresh like a desperate lovers' tryst
Wide ashen eyes turn to him, her lips ruby
How alluring she looks, a true madonna
Unknowingly, the queen of all succubi
King Wrenfrey leans forward to taste nirvana
But not her lips does he take, to her forehead
She's not for a tryst in the belladonna

   "Apologies if I scared you or caused dread,"
He speaks gently to the angel called Angel
    "Please understand what I did and what I said
    'Twas for the good of all. To God, I'm faithful
    A sacrifice saved, and evil's nest burned down
    Our duty to rid the world of the baneful."

Angel looks at him, eyes in which he could drown
With a shaky smile, she nods to King Wrenfrey
Gifting him a sight to beat others' renown
Enchanted by Angel pet's strength to obey
    "King and flower." The Hand creeps now from the wood
    "We return to our Majesty, her next play."

Five points of the pentagram, where the Hand stood
Encase our two leads, with nary more to fill
Leaving behind the burning witch hut for good
Wrenfrey thinks on as they press through the swamp swill
Finally finished with this little plan's stitch

There was no doubt he'd succeed, it was God's will
Our king's Lord demands the burning of the Witch
And while the woman was nowhere to be seen
Now Krios can't get aid from the Devil's bitch
The honourless man, seeker of the obscene
Would no doubt be on look out for advantage
His pox-filled heart seeking out familiar scene

But thanks to Frey, hawk-eyed with highest vantage
He sees all to come, sees us in the distance
The sight of him, near more than we can manage

Burn the house to the ground! You will find no resistance
Journey forth, and witness the reward of persistence

CHAPTER 9

The Hand says not a word; the troupe is silent
Their journey back to their Majesty's domain
In our king's head there's nothing more violent
Done the first task, back from realms of the insane
Should be jumping for joy, in awe and delight
Danger abounding, our king stood twixt the twain

But as their feet fly like His angels in flight
Over the clouds, over the people below
Not a word of gratitude about his plight

They enter the queen's halls, greeted by a glow
The fire from candelabra lighting splendour
Like Angel's hair in wind, flames dance to and fro
His fair Angel, the finest of her gender
Wall to wall of these halls hang noble portraits
Painted by the best, women soft and slender
Each detail captured their immortalized fates
Yet by a peasant girl they are put to shame
True to her name, an angel versus primates

He grabs her hand, desperate to touch her frame
Nerves on her shoulders dissipate with a sigh
A thankful smile thrown his way makes his knees lame

Think straight, our lusty king. Others are nearby
See the doors with flower encircled by snakes?
The same as the box, the mark of your ally

Like before, a single look causes heartaches
Sadness and vengeance radiating quite strong
The servants on either side, the power wakes
Promises whisper through their minds like birdsong
Goading them forth as they open the large door
And the dutiful Hand moves the two along
Staring up at the queen on her throne once more
Her demonic veil floating, mind of its own
Through it they feel her gaze, forming on them hoar

   "Noble queen, we return with the first keystone,"
Our true royalty speaks, lifting the box proud
     "Not just that, we have decimated the crone
     Set fire to her home, her patron surely cowed
     Foul ingredient, component, concoction
     Now all smoke for the Lord, all's left is a cloud
     Whisked away by the breeze, her soul on auction
     And in the insanity, a child was found
     On her way to a glorious adoption
     Thanks to the efforts of the best king around
     All went according to plan, my fairest queen
     Now to celebrate, wine, food, trumpets abound."

But there are no trumpets, no foods, no wine seen
Just an ice cold gaze that incinerates them
And a veil through which nothing our king can glean
The Hand bow, their loyalty a priceless gem
And the man Angel calls Titan steps forward
    "All as you said, our queen, thorns were cut from stem
    Made to look pristine, delicate, here onward
    Working against its nature, more to behold
    But now, at the least, to touch is less awkward."

Our Wrenfrey knows not what the queen was just told—
By her subordinate who speaks in riddle
Whether recommendation for praise or scold
He cares not about the warrior's spittle
Let him speak in a poor man's poetic verse
Let the queen feel smart with the tarradiddle
So long as they help to free him of his curse
Our king's patience will be worth its weight in gold
After all, he'd hate for fortunes to reverse

The Majesty, weeping angel, statue cold
Beckons forth, "Fallen king, show me what you've done
    Where is my mark, retrieved from where souls were sold?"

Blades in his ears from her voice, but like God's son
No torment was too much to do his duty
In terms of honour he was second to none
Lifting the box for all to see such beauty
Here lies their future, war with his betrayer
The tutoring queen to become his tutee

"Empty it."

Bewilderment at the suggestion's sayer
Our king turns to Angel, Angel to our king
He returns with a smile, the woman-slayer
    "To witness the immoral is a man's thing
    My lady, perhaps you know not the contents
    Not for the faint of heart, this evil I bring."

A chill in the air, his soul suffers, segments
The queen, hem of her dress like smoke, voice glacia
    "I know. For I placed what's there. End the pretense."

Angel turns to our king, our king to Angel
Without word, he empties the box's foul cargo
A putrid splat, they hold back sick as able
Gyrating upon the floor, organs bestow—
Their slithering, seizuring, sickening meat
Eagerly, they put on their unholy show
The queen's dress, hem of smoke, glides from 'neath her feet
Descending over her throne's stairs like water
It envelops the organs, feels the heartbeat

The entrails calm, almost as if they sought her
Amazed by her work, our king is here to stay
While Angel wonders if they're lambs to slaughter

    "Your next task," the queen speaks, no moment to pray
    "Three royal men stand between you and your goal

A king with two sons: one to rule, one to bray—
The unfairness of second born as his role
In the vault of their keep lies my mark once more
Only the king may open, none can extol—
Their way into the vault, make it past the door
A king you shall need and a king you shall get
My Hand will lead you, escort you to their shore."

Our king is already assessing the threat
To deal with one on this level, he needs tact
Royalty is smart, bold, make danger their pet
To acquire the Majesty's lost artifact
He'll have to summon all his cunning and guile
Take care of any attention he'd attract

   "Queen of untold grace, I accept your trial,"
Our king, how he continues to impress us
His voice powerful, his body fit, fine smile
A man of quality, he's here as our truss
It's good there's enough of him to go around
Oh! What a racket we would cause, what a fuss

But end our daydreaming, more words for the crowned
Our king speaks: "Fair queen, I'll do as you instruct
   Come divinity's angel or low Hell's hound
   But an answer, if I may, from your mind plucked
   What is it that we seek in this royal vault?
   Pray tell, what object are we sent to abduct?"

At once the room changes, calm grinds to a halt
Angel sees her breath in the new frigid air
And knows as she shivers, our king is at fault
But the queen is still, just a change in her stare
Slowly stripping the flesh from their frozen bones
'Til they match the pile of entrails by the stair

Our observant king, sensing the shift in tones—
Places his arm 'round Angel's shivering form
What little heat that's theirs, they share what they own

    "The *object*," the queen drags the word, a coiled swarm
    "You will find in the vault, naught more I will say
    Do as need demands of you, what keeps you warm
    You will rise above masses of lowly prey
    You will conspire with allies to take what's yours
    You will do what you know is right, it's your play
    But should you go astray, return on all fours
    Beg my forgiveness, implore my acceptance
    Let the mortification seep from your pores

    Plead your sin before us all, show us your repentance
    And we will listen and debate our acquiescence."

CHAPTER 10

There is darkness and day, there is dawn and dusk
Never do their feet tire, nor their lungs lose breath
The Hand's ready to defend down to the husk
Their charges wander between them, safe from death
The man creeps his arm around the woman's waist
Opening his mouth, all hear his shibboleth
    "Once Krios is defeated, his line disgraced
    I will show off your beauty to my homeland
    So all may be in envy of my fine taste
    Angel, you shall witness my glory firsthand
    To be treasured above all else at my side
    Family at your side, better future planned
    The sights you shall see, your grace will override
    A delight to have you amidst my castle
    I cannot toss you away once done this ride."

Angel can't help her laugh, comes without hassle
This man, she enjoys his enthusiasm
Like a boy, but dressed up with tact and tassel
Resting her head against him, a phantasm—
Creeps over her like a protective darkness

Titan, his thoughts an unreachable chasm
Gaze felt through veil, on her, she feels a starkness
Like she is as bare as a babe in the wood
Taking after his loved queen with his sharpness

But before its meaning can be understood
The clash of swords, shouts of the disenfranchised
Ahead, a young man is in need of some good
Two giants, equal to the Hand in sheer size
Dressed in hunter's leathers, expressions of hate
Swinging their weapons at the man they've surprised
The man who barely fends off his headless fate
But soon to accept if naught is done to help
His coat decorated with more than its plait

   "Hold now," our king says. "Of my kin is that whelp
   Not by blood, but class, a man who stands above
   Rescue to ensue, the answer to his yelp
   Let us not tarry, we've thugs to get rid of
   Go, my warriors, cut down the criminal
   Show me the reason behind your fair queen's love."

The Hand does as told, the judgement critical
Shadows devouring the sun, snuffing the light
Steps leaving black fire, following principle
Each second they grow larger, monsters of blight
Their dark weapons curl, hiss, scream, minds of their own
Steel souls hungry, singing for the blood of wight
Marching to their targets, eyes for them alone
To do what they must do for this old story

Like plagues, they descend, the next seeds to be sow
The bandits struggle, desperate for their quarry
But they're overwhelmed by their split attention
Soon to be naught but a memento mori
Their eyes find Angel pet's midst the contention
Death gurgles of one are followed by the next
Etched into her brain, from now 'til ascension

But our proud protector hides her from guilt's hex
Held to his side as they come to their new friend
Pools of red still pumping from nameless subjects

A man, no more than twenty, breaths on the mend
His bright eyes and toothy grin are infectious
He grabs our king's forearm to greet and commend,
    "Brother, you've saved that which I find most precious
    Namely me and my hide, which I don't take light!
    God is with me to be found in this nexus
    Away from my home, I travelled for a sprite
    Missing her childhood favourites I search the weald
    But come up empty-handed, try as I might
    Further and further I looked, through every field
    For a flower of a certain appearance

    But wandered too far, and I feared my fate sealed
    Upon me, two bandits with no adherence—
    To the common decency of man and God
    Disjointed even with their own coherence
    Offered all I had, enough gold to be awed
    But not even a glance spared, their weapons out

No wonder they're dead men with their plan so flawed
I thank you, friend, sent by Him I have no doubt
To have saved my life you've earned august favour
From my father, king of this land, with your bout
Yet my mission for the woman I savour—

Nay, hold, look there by the body of the thief
The flower! Let my good luck never waver."

Growing in a bath of crimson, stem and leaf
Drinking up life to give life to its petals
Impossible beauty pulled from disbelief
Had it always been there, amongst the nettles?
And lo, more than at first glance it's realized
The flower from the queen's seal! Raise your fettles

But the Hand's gone, to the surroundings, disguised
Their deed done, to their true function they move on
To observe, the ex-king to be analyzed

Our king speaks, "To save you from Lucifer's spawn—
    Is what anyone would do for his brethren
    As a fellow royal, least in days foregone
    I'll accompany you, as a veteran—
    Of surviving my own near-death banditry
    We can recount until our minds are barren."

The bright young man nods. "My life you've handed me
    You are honoured guests, you and your companion
    And as Prince of this land, none will disagree

My own gratitude overflows a canyon
Let us take our leave from such unsightliness
Enough to make your lady's calm abandon."

His hand brings Angel's to his lips. Knightliness—
Is never in short supply amongst these men
It fills her heart with a certain sprightliness
A brush of a kiss before he's on again
    "Come, let us hear the stories of the other
    On our way to the safety of my home's den
    'Fore the woods decide to put up a pother
    And spew forth more ill-intentioned foragers
    Fret not the inconvenience, it's no bother."

A sight to see, the Prince and two foreigners
Ushered along, arm around Angel pet's waist
Away from the bodies now Death's voyagers
The royals prattle, personal accounts chased
While the angel called Angel turns her head back
One last look at the bodies, fates interlaced

A new form has joined them, frail, old, and a face pain-wracked
Finger raised, they point at her, and she feels herself crack

CHAPTER 11

There are people everywhere, yet it's lifeless
The shrouds have followed from the Majesty's court
Anonymous faces veiled in her likeness
Moving 'round as peasant and sailor from port
Working as carpenter, watchman, and blacksmith
Begging for scraps as tramps with no last resort

Whatever their given roles, they move forthwith
With pulsing sound and indistinguishable—
Language, challenging God with its monolith
Collapsing under weight, extinguishable
These people pulled from the wreckage what was left
Others' understanding diminishable

Our king guides Angel before she's left bereft
A hand on her as they follow their lodestar
To the keep on the horizon, movements deft
His lips tickle her ear. "More and more bizarre
This little adventure which we find ourselves
Their shrouds. I wonder at what the meanings are
Maybe tradition from old books on their shelves

Regional practice with context lost to time."
Our king grows silent as if in thought he delves
Only to smile like a boy hiding his crime
    "Or perhaps executioner garb is in
    And I'm showing my age has long passed its prime."

Levity is welcome. Angel mirrors his grin
Those around vanish into the atmosphere
And soon they find themselves in the keep's within
Servants rush, dusting and washing windows clear
Spectacles that cast colours with their stained glass
Depictions of Mary and her son held dear
The Prince boasts himself before the lower class
His guests he's eager to impress. "Behold, friends
    A more splendorous vista none could amass
    Witness my home, whose eminence never ends
    Alive in its own right, with much character
    Pens history with these halls, comfort it lends
    Paintings on the walls give voice as narrator
    Never to grow dull, I find myself honoured
    To be given this home as a heritor
    But enough about that, let us move onward
    To meet the King and Queen, my parents on high
    Pleased, no doubt, to have their petitions bothered
    By the saviour of their son, their new ally."

Our king's chest puffs out, soon to be recognized
In a place not competing with a pigsty
Krios' fall has already been canonized

In bold paintings and brave literary works
All to be displayed in his home, patronized

To the throne room, they go to enjoy their perks
Wrenfrey bulling through, Angel dodging servants
Her care for them, one of her lovable quirks

Through large doors, they find the royal observants
Listening to the common man's petitions
Serfs lined up, coming like an ocean's currents
To demand the royals be the physicians—
To their simple lives' problems, never-ending
Can't pay tax, stolen goats, lacking ambitions

But now their day can brighten, greed suspending
As they see our king and his Angel enter
The Prince announcing to all ears attending,
    "Mother! Father! I return from Hell's centre
    My body to be chopped away from my head
    But thanks placed in he who killed my tormentors
    Before you, he who reattached my life's thread
    And his companion to challenge the seraphs
    With her beauty, eyes of grey and hair of red
    Break now from your talks of increasing tariffs
    And bestow upon them all that I've assured
    Let the peasants be handled by your sheriffs."

But the King and Queen, their good will is not lured
The King especially gives a look to hew—

Even the strongest, their audacity cured
His words firm as he speaks, "What have we told you
    About interrupting us in our duties
    With your flights of fancy and make-believe spew?"

The shocked face of the Prince, cheeks red as rubies
No longer the proud man from before, boasting
But a little boy, captured for girls to tease
Lost ability for witty riposting
Tongue tied, he forces out, "But this time it's true!
    From brigands they saved me, the guests I'm hosting."

But the King slams his fist, giving ire's preview
    "Enough! Just like your damnable Greek heathens
    Making up stories when there's real work to do."

Whispers, snickers, trail through the crowd like demons
Peasants watch, and though their faces are shrouded
It's easy to see their grins, each like lesions—
Across the Prince's pride, his cognition clouded
As he's suddenly drenched in the strong feeling
Of this place being one man overcrowded

His mother, the Queen, with a speech appealing
Attempts to patch a threadbare relationship
But more than mere words are needed for healing
    "You can tell us later, my little parsnip
    Your father and I must attend to our tasks
    As is the charge all royalty must equip
    Happiness of the people where true strength basks

Each one a sibling, to lift up and care for
Attention properly given when one asks
But we must be fair, lest others demand more
You'll have your time, but now is for another
Go, entertain your friends with your Greek folklore."

With that, both turn away, father and mother
They no longer acknowledge the Prince red-faced
While Angel and our king look at each other
This whole interaction leaving a bad taste

With pained quiet, the Prince ushers out his guests
Shoulders slumped, 'fore the whole court he was disgraced
His back to them. It is where Angel's hand rests
Her lips part to speak but he turns with a smile
Too bright, too wide, as if all were simple jests

"Perhaps later you two may build your profile—
With my parents. Until then, stay with us here
The guest chambers, follow me somewhere worthwhile."
He moves at once, confidence back in his sphere
"No doubt the room will be the finest you've seen
No expense spared. Those are the rules I adhere
Thick blankets, down-stuffed pillows, robes byzantine
For he who saved the world a day of mourning
He deserves something bordering on obscene."
They stop before oak slabs. "But word of warning
Past these doors, you may not be able to leave
Once you have taste of your new life aborning."

Just then laughter gives the affluence reprieve
A sleeved arm wraps its way around the Prince's head
By a man of similar build, to relieve—
The two guests of the bluster that the Prince spread
With sharp eyes and an easy smile that melts hearts
In terms of looks, this family is well-fed

   "Kin of kings but the posturing of upstarts,"
The bewitching man speaks with a voice to match
   "What does he drone about now? His gold or smarts?
   My brother is not one to let silence catch
   When he could fill it with the greatness of him
   But as the second, you need some itch to scratch
   Not that I know, I don't have a life to skim
   A life of hardships, of doing not what's fair
   But of what's right for all, no matter how grim
   My destiny, the destiny of the Heir!
   And constantly wishing to steal some thunder
   That destiny, the destiny of the spare
   Is that not right, my dearest baby brother?"

His laughter fills the halls, the Prince is red hot
Releasing himself from his brother's smother
The newcomer eyes the two his brother caught
Frey matching the intensity of his stare
Angel, her hand grabbed, and a kiss placed as taught

   "I overheard your exploits, answered prayer,"
The newcomer says, "As Heir, I invite you

A feast prepared for my parents' favourite pair
Held tonight, you'll be guests of honour, prime view
To witness the spare equal himself a fool
When one such lady appears in his purview."

The Prince stills, uncaring of the ridicule
"She's coming so soon? I've no time to prepare!
A woman of her grace, the ultimate jewel."

The Heir chuckles, happy with his little scare
"Have no fear. With me there she'll know no one more
All others will fade when it's my breath we share."

The Prince's teeth grind as the proud Heir leaves their door
With laughter piercing the air, intentions done
The Prince turns to his guests, forgotten rapport
"Thousand apologies. That was less than fun
Please, enjoy your room or feel free to traverse
I will summon you when the feast has begun
For now, I must..." He pats his coat with a curse
"It's gone! My flower! My gift for my lady!
And she comes soon, this could not get any worse
On the floor, lost in the excitement, maybe
Perpetually foiled, but it must be 'round."
The Prince pouts, looking less royal more baby

Angel wants to help, but she's picked off the ground
In the arms of our king like a bride come home
And he gives some advice to his fellow crowned

"Keep eyes on your things 'lest they get up and roam."
Then our king and his Angel are inside, free
Finally, the door shuts on that little gnome

So simple a task. This was all going so easy
As our goodly king plans the next step in his crime spree

CHAPTER 12

To attend a party of the upper class
A certain presentation is essential
We know, and some of us are lower than grass!

Sadly, there are those not experiential
Uncouth speech and sense of fashion offending
In need of help to reach their full potential
It's here one specific angel, descending
Casts our king glances as she tries on dresses
A crinkle on her brow, in need of mending
　　"I know nothing of this," Angel expresses
　　"Sashes, corsets, with layer upon layer
　　How I'm to blend in this night of excesses—
　　A mystery for some zealous soothsayer
　　Let me stay in here, I'll only embarrass
　　I don't wish to hear the words from naysayers."

Our king, all-powerful, rise like Nereus
Comes to the aid of woman's fragility
His man's thoughts to relax his future Doris
　　"My Angel, you doubt your capability

To stun rooms with mere seconds of your presence
Rid yourself of your serf culpability
On my arm you'll know only people's pleasance
None will know of your past or inner working

It will be our secret, and their misfeasance
Now, so I don't feel like I'm a boy lurking
Allow me to venture out, to find someone—
More able to assist you," he says, smirking

With a smile, Angel says, "Frey, my thanks is won
I'm sure none will deny such a sad request
To help a grown woman get her dressing done."

Our king laughs. He holds humour close to his breast
Tenderly, he captures a lock of her hair
And upon its crimson strands, a kiss is pressed
"Careful, unless my heart you wish to ensnare,"
A whisper on the lock, sending up shivers
Anticipation, promise, want without care

Then he's gone, leaving his girl with her quivers
Eager to join this feast, enjoy the party
With good food to eat and brew to drown livers
Too much to hope they were fans of Astarte?
Feels like ages, too long since his last conquest
It's needed for mortal men to stay hearty
At least now our king's advancing in his quest
A woman of some calibre he must find
To make sure this night ends smoothly, not in jest

There! He sees one, delicate hands intertwined
Her snow white hair and her eyes, rubies of blood
Ethereal, empyreal, too refined

Why does looking upon her hurt, his heart flood?
Weakness for a woman to render him so
His legs stride him forth, as if through thickest mud
    "Maiden, in whose red eyes I see Heaven's glow
    And whose beauty would cause royal men to war
    I introduce myself as one such man's foe."

Our great king bows, ready to collect his score
For this woman to assist with woman things
He speaks, "I ask for help for one I adore
    Like you, an angel merely missing her wings
    But unlike you, lacking sophistication
    Scary their kind finds the ways of queens and kings
    Plucky but infantile is their vocation
    But I need not tell you, their minds capable—
    Of only complaining about taxation."

Our king laughs, his humour inescapable
The doll before him tilts her head, a small smile
Her voice comes out, her allurement palpable
    "Perhaps if you put your mind in theirs a while
    There's good reason to find royalty scary
    When lords act as peers at a farmer's trial."

His amusement clearly shared by this faerie
Our king places her hand upon his arm's crux
Lead her to her new duty, not to tarry

But alas, stopped by one of her suitor fucks
The Prince, running to them, eyes bright and grin wide
A man slightly better than the common schmucks
The Prince speaks, "My lady, I missed you outside
     I'm so pleased to see you. How long has it been?
     Nearing half a decade has made me cockeyed."

The lady gives a curtsey to the Prince seen
She says, "I missed you amongst the growing crowd
     Servants, guests, family, but no you between
     Not one for large assembly I left in shroud
     To explore our old playground in solitude
     Relive times when imagination's not cowed
     Only then to have my attention pursued
     By this lord at my side, a favour he's asked
     To help his lady and earn his gratitude."

The Prince nods. "Then you must do as you've been tasked
     If your heart holds any affection for me
     As the man at your side is why I've not passed
     An attack. I heard the cry of the banshee
     Saved my life, he did, so we may reunite
     He made our future an actuality."

The waxen-haired lady holds her gasp of fright
She frees herself from our king, goes to her Prince

"Are you okay, my old friend? Are you all right?
As I touch your head, I notice your sharp wince
What is the reason for your tempting of fate?
And your flowery words, you better not mince."

The Prince chuckles. "Worry not, I'll tell you straight
    At the feast tonight when I recount the tale
    To a captive audience, each word with weight
    Now do as our hero wants, every detail
    Later I shall gather you up for a dance
    Enjoy one's company, as male and female."

The fair lady scoffs, immune to his gaze's trance
    "Later then. Excuse me, as I venture out
    To have my own damsel-in-distress romance."

    "In the guest hall," our king gives a helpful shout
Both watch as she disappears 'round the corner
    "Careful with that one, Prince, have no room for doubt
    Lest you be your masculinity's mourner
    Women are keen to prey on uncertainty
    Be strong, lest they run off with some foreigner."

The Prince shakes his head, "Looks of Aphrodite—
    But the devotion of the mother of Christ
    In her, I'm as sure as in God Almighty."

Our king speaks, in deep thought for his coming heist
    "A woman like that is a commodity
    Perhaps my reward should be her, fairly priced."

The young man pulls back, losing comradery
He grabs his thumping heart as his face grows pale
He can't comprehend the request's oddity
The Prince speaks, "We should chat more over some ale
    I can recommend something more worth your time
    Your prize is not something I wish to curtail
    Besides, as prince of a kingdom in its prime
    There's much we can talk about, opulence-wise
    To be silent would certainly be a crime."

But our king remains adamant. "For my prize—
    The maid of ivory hair and complexion
    I wonder if it matches between her thighs..."

    "No!" The Prince shouts but makes a quick correction
    "I mean, she will have no part in this dealing
    You choose anything, except her perfection
    We're sure to find you something more appealing
    Than another woman for you to deal with."
He ends with a chuckle, a nervous feeling

Ever one step ahead, our king, the wordsmith
Gives a long sigh, his defeat deeply present
All is building up to his clever plan's pith
He speaks, "As you say, Prince, despite my lament
    Oh, what a woman she would be at my side
    My prize would need to triple to make a dent
    What could possibly replace her as my bride?
    Wait, a thought springs to mind of a certain seal

Snakes and a flower, your king's vault where they hide
Grand idea, Prince! I accept your new deal
Retrieve for me what's sealed with flower and snake
Do this and my bid for the girl I'll repeal."

The Prince is stark. "What you seek you must forsake
Only the king may open, no exception
What's inside leaves only rumours in its wake
But I know this: to take it is reception—
Of a terrible death for the sitting king
For he's the guardian since its inception
My father, the King, won't let you pull this string
And should he pass, my brother would be the same

It's pathetic, my role as second offspring
The only one with sanity to his name
With no fear of some ridiculous old curse
Reduced to sitting upon my hands in shame
Forgive me, my friend, again I must coerce—
To wish for something easier to attain

But let it be after the feast we converse
So many treasures: gold, land, titles to gain
We are sure to find one that suits your great deed
For now, the festivities. Let pleasure reign."

With that, he turns and leaves our king with his greed
But our patient king, with tightened white knuckles
He's thinking of how to have his plan succeed

But then his gaze caught, his vexation buckles
There, resting on the floor, a certain flower
    "What do we have here?" Our king of kings chuckles

He grabs it by the stem, sensing a hidden power
If the damned vault needs a king, a king it will devour

CHAPTER 13

The haunting sounds of the psaltery and harp
Play for an audience unappreciative
Used to the music, used to flaunt and look sharp
Their privileges never depreciative
Their titles allow authority to rule
While their riches ensure the prerogative
Our king is at home in this fortune cesspool
It feels like each person, a ghost from his past
His people! Dressed in fur, gold-thread, and jewel
Nearby, the Heir chitchats with those of his caste
Their eyes meet, to the other they raise their cup
The Heir's grin is wide, with thankfulness steadfast

Our king has to hold back a laugh at the pup
Words in the right ear, flowery suggestion
He can't wait to see the troubles he's stirred up

Just then, strangers from 'mongst the room's congestion
Two, a man and woman, come to our king's side
The young man speaks, "Ah, the eternal question
Do I enjoy myself, berth to others wide

Or do I mingle, blowing smoke up asses
Of those already with blackened tongues supplied?"

Our king swirls his drink, eyes about the masses
The Heir teasing the Prince with light-hearted jabs
Parents, King and Queen, laughing at the sasses
Queen pats the Prince's cheek, consoling for the stabs
While the King and Heir enter deep discussion
As our king's bait, the Heir reaches for and grabs

Our great king responds without repercussion
    "As you've approached me, you must've picked the latter
    Shall I squat to ease your bellow's percussion?"

Laughter emits from the guest of the chatter
Tearing our king's attention from the royals
Greeting him with more temping subject matter
    "Good to keep him in check lest ego spoils,"
The lady speaks with a smile brightly aglow

The man's eyes roll, "Go join your fellow gargoyles."

Our king studies them, focus on just one though
Both share a similar face as their own's base
But with hers, sultry chocolate eyes overflow
Beauty marks beneath them, gaze makes the heart race
Arching eyebrows, heart-shaped lips slightly parted
Necklace dips between her full breasts, the scapegrace
Eager invitation to lands' uncharted

Her raven hair looking one pin from chaos
Atop her head, wish for release wholehearted

Our king's fingers itch, captured in her pathos
Between this siren and the white-haired goddess
Gorgeous girls must be part of the crown ethos

Our faithful king pulls his gaze from her bodice
    "Forgive my crassness before such a vision
    Whose beauty brings to their knees a whole caucus
    My whole self unfit for such imprecision."

To which the Aphrodite smiles in pleasure
And he turns back to the man for revisions:
    "Regret and bad manners in equal measure
    Pray, perhaps tell me who is the inviter—
    Of you, fine gent, and this absolute treasure."

The man chuckles with a grin, the mood lighter
But there is something about him, coiled sheeting
Like black powder waiting for an ignitor
The young man speaks, "Forgive me my first greeting
    I'm a guest and Friend of our prince, second-born
    Since our birth's day, our friendship never fleeting
    It is a tale for the ages I forewarn
    Together always, close as blood, thick as thieves
    Allegiance to the other forever sworn
    Oh, and he'd test it too, with tricks up his sleeves
    Taking hold of noble women not his own
    With that pretty face, female hearts beg reprieves

Of course, no plan goes as planned. His often blown
And I'd be left to take care of the husbands
When they come to use his head as their grindstone
What good times we had, then and now, truly grand
My brother, we share all we have between us
Testament to our families, we withstand
But more about him, my Twin loves to discuss
Look now at her eyes, see her gaze is forlorn
How she dreams of receiving a single buss."

The woman sputters, her goodwill is well worn
He can't contain his laughter at her cheeks' red
    "Shut your mouth, you churl," she says to her side's thorn

As the siblings bicker, our king lifts his head
Chatter picks up, heads bob to see who's arrived
Excusing himself, he rushes on ahead
To the front of the buzzing crowd, he's revived
By the sight of purity before his eyes

For too long, our great king knows he's been deprived
Angel and the white-haired girl elicit cries
From the women, they lament the unfairness
From the men, they pray for their chance to arise
A chance they'd ne'er receive, lacking awareness—
That they were already claimed by better men

Our vainglorious king moves to his rareness
Angel looks like one of his station's women

In a dress reminiscent of princesses
More fitting than her rags from her home's pigpen

Our king stops before her, lauding her tresses
The Prince mirroring them with his white-haired one
They each take their woman's arm, free of stresses
As they walk to their seat, silence is undone
Angel's voice pipes up, "Frey, did you see that girl?
    With ashen hair and her eyes' blood overrun
    She helped me to dress, the daughter of an earl
    But does she not appear familiar to you?
    Like her from before, whose life we did unfurl?
    Yet I... I feel there's more trying to break through."

But our king shakes his head as he adores her
Guiding her to her seat for the feast on cue
Wrenfrey speaks, "It matters not, I don't demur
    What does is you and your pure Hebe effect
    Stunning all 'round you, everyone will concur
    Jealousy of me as I hold what's perfect
    Their envy gives me new strength, necessary—
    As my life, you're sure to grant, I must protect
    You're more beautiful than that white-haired faerie
    You're more dazzling than the Twin of the Friend
    You're more everything than the Virgin Mary."

She gulps, waiting for lightning to be their end
The blasphemy is unheard by those around
Angel finds herself captured in our king's wend

His lips caress her fingers, the touch profound
Promise in his hooded stare makes her breaths fast
Until they are interrupted by the crowned

"Hear me, hear me, put down what food you've amassed!"
The King at the table's head, taking a stand
The Queen, with endless golden hair, his contrast
The rotund man speaks, with his tankard in hand
   "To the surprise of none, I have become old
   Mere waiting for one of you to act your brand
   And kill me off to gain a further foothold."
Roaring laughter follows the King's jesting speech
He continues: "But as none of you are bold
   I must find my son, your future king, a peach
   Of the utmost stock, the zenith of her breed
   A woman of intelligence I beseech
   To smooth out the foolhardy things he's decreed."
More howls, playful shoving of the laughing Heir
   "But such a rare creature, how could I succeed?
   All was lost, country's future up in the air
   Until a thought came to me moments before—
   This feast upon which you gorge, I do declare
   My son's wife, future queen, for all to adore
   Sitting just there, her parents in agreement
   A certain white-haired dame is now spoken for."

At once, feasters are buzzing with excitement
All around the table there's a sense of cheer
Chatter of weddings, new sense of enjoyment

The woman with blood eyes, her shock is sincere
Face as pale as her hair as the Heir comes forth
On one knee he goes, his voice is loud and clear
    "With all my heart, I will fill your days with mirth
    Bride, as queen expect no less than you deserve
    From afar, I've watched your time upon this Earth
    And now, bound together, I hope to preserve—
    That joy upon your face, calm upon your brow
    From this single moment there is no recurve
    You belong to me and myself to you now
    Let there be no doubts of our new partnership
    All here bear witness, I make the solemn vow
    My only regret is the lacking courtship
    But have our whole lives not had a courtship's bliss?
    I know you'll come to recognize our kinship."

And there, upon her hand, he places a kiss
The adoration of the crowd for their lord
Loosing content sighs for the man and his miss

And then there's the swirling blackness, untoward
From the Prince tendrils of darkness radiate
Slimy and sick, they writhe of their own accord
Leaving behind their sludge, disease incarnate
Reaching, he will not lose her, he will not lose!
The Prince is blind with desires to suffocate
Ire is a black hole, work of the Devil's muse
A stain spreading thick across the bitter end
Creeping over the Prince like living tattoos

The Heir continues, "Your troubles I will mend
   After all, who better to assume the role—
   Of your faithful husband than your faithful friend?"

Out pops a certain flower, stem, petals whole
Girl and blossom, beautiful works of nature
Admired by all around, the scene takes its toll
The Prince is wound tighter than a filature
As her delicate hand takes hold of the stem
Burned into his mind this evil portraiture
Sitting right beside, close enough to condemn
She's taken from him, yet all he does is bawl
Coward, he seethes as another paws his gem

His bravery is demonstrated for all
Pathetic. A waste. Unsuitable suitor
But our king, patient, wise, pats the Prince, his thrall
A quick gesture, from Devil to commuter
The Prince needs it, and he's going to need more
To distract from the brother he would neuter

And as the night carries on, a change in store
As dancing breaks out, she belongs to the Heir
While the Prince watches, thoughts of a Cain encore
Music caresses the guests, flits through the air
A headiness descends, minds mellowed with wine
As singles move to become a bonded pair
The King and his Queen, a bloodline of bloodlines
Hold one another close in hypnotic sway
For once slaves to the siren music's design

Nobles dance together, no worries to weigh
While shrouded servants are scurrying about
Cleaning and keeping sobriety at bay
Caring for burning incense, erasing doubt
Frankincense and jasmine, honey and lilac
Coalesce with music to satiate a drought—
Formerly subdued inside their hollow sack
Our king most of all, feeling appetite stir
His mark intoxicating in her attack

Angel attempts her best, with moves to deter—
Even the utmost experienced dancer
As she pulverizes, our king's feet concur
The man has seen less destruction from cancer
But the pull of her brow, the flush of her face
Makes him ignore, as he knows how to answer
      "Slow down, match my steps. I move and you give chase
      A tale as old as time we're bringing to life
      Follow your instincts. Slow down, it's not a race

      Deep breaths. Only I'm here. Free yourself of strife
      Float on the floor, press your body into mine
      Let loose this carnal tension that's been so rife."

His whispers in her ear, shivers down her spine
The heat of his breath upon her slender neck
Her heaving chest, thoughts begin to intertwine
His finger to her chin, to see her eyes beck
His touch scorches her throat, and over her heart
Her lips part, cheeks redden, embarrassed to check—

The expression of our king, so wise and smart
The music fades, the incense rolls in on mist
This fog is too much. Her mind needs to restart!

But there's no rest found, with a flick of his wrist
Twirl 'round and 'round, unable to concentrate
Whirlwind where sense and desire can't coexist
This battle his kind has mastered, it's innate
Decades of honing converge on this moment
Its purpose to overwhelm sanity's state
Angel pet the next victim of its intent
Her mind unable to fight off his bold eyes
Left to the mercy of what they represent

Desire coils with need, enough to agonize
As his dark gaze leaves a scorching trail of fire
Her dress catching in its flames, reaching the skies
Following prey, our king joins her in her pyre
Their steps in sync as they fly across the floor
Caressed by the music of the harp and lyre

His touch on her body makes her wish for more
But he lets his lips hover over her skin
Teasing, building, lusting, knowing what's in store
Their hooded eyes meet, his hand rests on her chin
She meets him halfway as ruby lips are kissed
Both ready for this night to truly begin

He lifts her up. He can no longer resist
Eager to set ablaze this slow burn desire

Ensure all is perfect and nothing is missed
Away with this night, its troublesome attire
Our king is done, focused only on one thing

To their room, he takes his Angel to retire
To strip her of the unyielding cloth and string
To place his lips upon her exquisite skin
To show her what it means to be with a king

The feast ends. All wander to sleep, in dream or its kin
Except shadows that fester, ready to gorge on sin

CHAPTER 14

It is still dark as they lay betwixt the sheets
Angel's hand on our king, softened by moonlight
Enjoying the calm in this house of elites
Her fingers trace his chest, so fragile and slight
Fatigue calls to them, entices them to sleep
And a peace descends as all around feels right

Knocks shatter! Under their door, the shadows creep
With a knowing chuckle, our king leaves their bed
To assist with a certain royal black sheep
He opens their door, bursting pride, high-born bred
A look of satisfaction upon his face
Gazing at two figures, pleasantries are shed

The Prince and his Friend, grimness surrounds their space
Our king steps forth, deliberate, expectant
The two turn, him to follow, another place
And he goes, winding through memories remnant
Shadowing their backs past familiar landscape
Desire for his lost castle ever present

They come to a stop under starry night's drape
Away from prying eyes and listening ears
In a pavilion of octagonal shape

Around, only willow trees and angel's tears
The hiss of the crickets and chill of the moon
Universe playing the music of the spheres
It's here that the Prince asks of his friends a boon

Voice shakes like his shoulders, "Humiliated,
     And my dear brother acts as if he's immune
     Father as well, my pride they mutilated
     They knew she was mine. It's been so since childhood
     Yet here they leave me, pathetic, castrated!"
He slams his fist against the pavilion wood
The anger echoing, pulsating outrage
     "I gathered you here to do what's right, what's good
     My dear Friend who's forever there to assuage
     To protect me from myself and my crazed plans
     A voice of reason far beyond any sage
     And you, my new guest, who saved me from Death's hands
     A stranger yet done more than my flesh and blood
     Council received, loud and clear across these lands
     Assist me and you will secure your heart's flood
     Riches, titles, women, all that you desire
     All that needs be done is to fix one small dud."

Our king, the brilliant man, looks at the young sire
Frenzy clings to him like women on our lord

Wild desperation stokes the Prince's inner fire
The Friend stands small, his sympathy in accord
An icy wariness has taken his form
Caution is there as he takes a step forward

From him spews nonsense, "I feel your mental storm
    For your one love to be ripped from you is rot
    A feat of aplomb I could never perform
    At the feast's announcement, my own heart was fraught!
    But I do confess, I fear your coming speech
    Do not suggest something that will make you naught."

As always, it appears our king has to teach
Young boys and their noble morals. It's so cute
It's time for our king to provide some outreach

    "Allow me to take that concern and transmute,"
He starts off, arms wide with a welcoming smile
    "What it should be is anger. Let it take root
    Our prince is more than aggrieved in this trial
    He's been disgraced before all who came this night
    His masculinity is what they defile
    Crush his manhood, want to take away his bite
    What good will a woman be to our Prince then?
    They trust him not to put up a decent fight."

The Prince is pulled, like his heart time and again
But as his Friend is hunched, his thin wrists displayed
Our great king stands tall, a paragon of men

In this scenario, who's better to aid?
The Friend prattles more, "Use your head, don't be rash
    This is your brother, the Heir, your hand be stayed
    Our Lord-in-Heaven, more than simple backlash
    More attention than I can divert, brother
    Remain level-headed before you're made ash
    Father is forfeit, but think of your mother
    The loss of two sons, don't condemn her to that
    That would be cruelty beyond any other."

The Prince pushes him away, done with this spat
    "Provide me solutions, not consequences!
    I brought you here to devise, not to chitchat
    My brother to suffer his recompenses
    He somehow stole my gift to her, risked my life—
    To find that which she wants past all expenses
    Flower as perfect as she, my future wife
    Now my brother wishes a taste of her lips
    But I promise only a taste of my knife."

Our king clasps his shoulder. "You must come to grips—
    With the reality of what you're asking
    There will be no turning back once the scale tips
    Ignore thoughts of him in her presence, basking
    His hands upon her, her eyes burning with lust
    Their bodies as one, virginal unmasking
    Forget his name in her sharp moans with each thrust
    The memory of you shrinking until gone
    Growing more desperate until both combust."

"Quiet!" The poor Prince shakes like a little fawn
His mind whirls, his heart aches, his breaths come too fast
Thoughts creep but twisting too quick to focus on

His Friend is here to speak, though nobody asked—
The opinion of this lowly yaldson fop
Nothing like our king, charming, tough, built to last
    "It's difficult, but this line of thought must stop
    A dangerous road, brother, please don't walk it
    People are always looking for heads to lop
    Your brother's wrong, his love for her counterfeit
    But yours is not! Would she like how you are now?
    Or when your eyes meet after your throat is slit?
    The end of her world, a sin you won't allow
    The murder of your brother, *of your brother*!
    Please, talk to your parents. He's no golden cow."

The speech ends and they stare at one another
Confliction cracks through the poor Prince's sure visage
Here comes the time now for our king to smother
    "The parents that cared not for their son's scrimmage—
    With two slaughterous brigands full of bloodthirst?
    Comfort of heartlessness is their privilege
    Even I, a newcomer, can see he's cursed
    I hear whispers from nobles who say it's so
    Even servants laugh at him 'til their lungs burst
    You call yourself friend, but say 'suffer in woe'
    Needless suffering, I say, take hold of fate
    Stop being understudy in the Heir's show!"
Our king's words pound the air, reinvigorate

The Prince is frothing, his anger returning
He shouts, "Laugh do they? Cursed? Those invertebrates!
    Their minds are feeble, judgement undiscerning
    Yes, yes, I... I remember how they snicker
    As I passed, their audacity was burning
    Their murmurs echo, from townsfolk to vicar
    And now they leave me with a final insult
    Believing I'll what? Drown myself in liquor?

    But I'll never give them the desired result
    No, I'll wrestle this town into submission
    Leaving those louts with only me to exult."

The wind has picked up its own apparition
Loud whistles through the pavilion speak to them
In frantic whispers, they beg for admission
Wriggling in his ears, trying to stop mayhem
But our king's cupidity is a redoubt
Protecting the birthright of his diadem

But the Friend has no strength, can't do it without
His face is solemn, his words drown in the wind
    "Good luck, brother. I pray for what's brought about."

The Prince is stunned to stillness, his friendship skinned
Watching as his Friend leaves, back growing smaller
Each step causes more memories to exscind
Childhood, the three of them, short but him taller
He and his Friend play with wooden sword and shield

She watches from the shade, their best extoller
Her white-hair distracts him from their battlefield
The beauty of her crimson eyes, spellbinding
With her sincere smile and laugh, hearts are revealed

Gone now, trampled under his Friend's foot, grinding
Years shredded before the poor Prince's very eyes
The perfect little puppet, our king's finding

    "Fear not, lad," Wrenfrey says. "You still have allies
    Not only will I stay by you, but plan all
    With your one job to carry out the demise
    A quagmire from my past gives the wherewithal
    An old wise man whispered me a formula
    From a man before him, that would cause one's fall
    One sip, ears ring from an off-key orchestra
    Vision goes red, uncontrollable fury
    Need to kill the closest, rip free viscera
    And better, no need to convince a jury
    The victim is to be gutted where they stand
    If only to defend from mindless flurry
    Gone mad from sun or a destiny too grand
    Who's to know your poor brother's addled last thought?

    But life moves on, all must continue as planned
    Free now to enjoy what your hard work has wrought
    Reflection mirrored in crimson irises
    White strands caressing your fingers, soft lips caught."

Our king's words infect the mind like viruses
The Prince nodding, free of the Friend's influence
He speaks, "Please, bestow me your dark sciences
    Anything will be yours, take my affluence
    Just help me rid my world of that wife-stealer
    Or else there's no need for life's continuance."

Our king stares into the eyes of the squealer
His whimpers overtaken by our king's voice,
    "You know what it is that I ask, the trade's her—
    For the prize from your family vault, your choice
    Should your callow mind find this vile, we end here
    But should we commence, then soon we both rejoice."

The Prince frowns. "I thought I had made myself clear
    Only the sitting king may open the vault
    It's a rule, to which even God must adhere."

Our king speaks thus, "The king *will* open the vault."
First there's confusion, then dawning clarity
The pale Prince gulps, "The king will open the vault."

Black umbra coils the wind with familiarity
Black as the shadows that defend a light's rarity

CHAPTER 15

Angel pet doesn't know that we can all see her
Watching our king from her willow hiding place
Rosy cheeks and plump lips make our innards purr
She can't hear our king's words, too far from the space
Yet, oddly, she feels wary coming nearer
She shouldn't stray far from the great willow's base

What would bring Angel out here? What would steer her?
Fear of being left out? Need to see her king?
Well, there he is! Our superb Judas mirror
His staff of life to make allegiances swing
To make others dance to his effortless tune
All with the idea it's their own they sing

Our king delves into the sad Prince's head to prune
So engrossed he doesn't see Angel pet is there
But we are, and lo, what shades does she commune?
The wind sheds silence, words trickle through the air,
 "What came first in this aftershock of events?
 Sordid results from one who stood without care."

Angel encased by a forest's enchantments
A sliver of fear as she looks for the source
Eerie speech that a croaking voice supplements
It speaks, "Who came first in this tale of remorse?
    A tale that leaves all heart-broken, just like her
    It was me, when I gave her shelter, of course
    I'm asked to hold a box with contents that stir
    By perplexity of blood and ivory
    Adult or child, I'm lost in memory's blur
    But the start when I opened my home blithely
    To a ghost my two Sons and I tried to warm
    That is the start, back when things were still lively
    Instead of cold limbo, purgatory's norm
    My heart's empty, but tries to care even more."
The hollow wind carries a willow leaf swarm

Angel pet is bound, transfixed down to her core
As the voice of this sad whatever is heard
Nothing like our king, oozing poise from each pore

Oh yes, we too hear the wind and willow's word
Dare not deign our lord with its significance
He's busy with other matters, undeterred

    "Who are you?" Angel asks of the dissonance
She fears the answer as much as the unknown
Wishing she'd stayed back, or at least vigilance

Willow shudders, great size of a trunk full grown
The voice comes, "I was a mother. I still am

Daughter stolen and Sons slain, I am alone
Weaker with each loss until weak as a lamb
I lose myself to grief and yet here I stay
With each time, each time, like a battering ram
To witness my children but from far away
Stuck on this plane to watch again and again
Always the same, the same, never a new day
Who came first in this tale of fallen women?
It was her, of course, when she rode in on Death
Spinning augury, a stranger beyond ken

And now I'm trapped, trapped amongst the baby's breath
In a never-ending cycle of despair
To be as unremembered as third son, Seth
I want nothing but happiness. This I swear
Not mine, but my children's. Rage to disappear
I'll do all I can, my afterlife I'll spare
Oh, child, are you a puppet or puppeteer?
What mask do you wear this time, writer or pawn?
What is your role, to prove a point or endear?
And who is it all for? Yourself? Your heart's brawn?
Nevertheless, I'm here, I'm here, my daughter
I hope this story gives you strength to move on."

Angel loses the binding spell that caught her
The willow leaves kiss her as she dashes through
A promise to meet come Hell and high water
Her head confused, her understanding askew
Running back to the safety of the castle
Where her king, our king, enjoys his night anew

In the halls, past the columns, this girl gracile
Into the chambers where our great king awaits
A bright smile comes to his face without hassle
In his arms he lifts her, his joy dominates
 "Wonderful news to share, my fair paramour
 But first I'm to know where you were in such straits
 Gone from my bed, face pale, a sight I abhor
 Even now you're shaking, tell me what you saw
 What's disturbed you so? Must I even a score?"

He sets her down, waiting for her nerves to thaw
A few breaths to calm down with little success
She tries, even as chittering aches her jaw
She says, "I cannot say what I saw in stress
 For I saw nothing but the wind and willow
 But a voice, truly, please, one it does possess!
 The voice spoke to me in riddles that burrow

 Lost children, puppeteers, an endless cycle
 I know not if it's from above or below
 Deliverance by the archangel, Michael
 Or this be one of foul Lucifer's cheap tricks
 Clawing for a decent soul to recycle

 Yet I know this isn't for the crucifix
 The voice firmly in the middle yet neither
 Oh, these feelings well up even you can't fix
 Ravage the heart and mind, leaving no breather
 Oh Wrenfrey, I don't think we should stay this path
 Let us run away from here, leave this seether."

He speaks, "You're scared. Join me for a soothing bath,"
He caresses her hair, amusement growing
There's no hysteria quite like women hath

She stands before him, behind moonlight glowing
Her worry is clear, her grey eyes wide as discs
    "Please listen, my lord, there is danger flowing
    I can't explain but we must beware the risks
    A wiggling thought in my head I can't grasp
    Reaching closer, but each time away it whisks
    What if this course leads to your crown and your asp?
    I don't like this, please, we can start life anew
    Away from the queen's dark magic and its rasp."

His brow lifts, listening to madness debut
Then he speaks, "All this... due to a talking tree?"
Angel's mouth slams shut. He believes her untrue

Getting to his feet, ignoring Angel's plea
He stretches out his delicious back muscles
    "A trick of the mind that causes you to flee."
Our strong king answers her distress with chuckles
    "Don't let this silliness stain your pretty head
    You're too delicate to be marred by troubles
    It is my lot in life, my line born and bred
    To deal with the stresses of cerebration
    Planning more than the simple harvest ahead
    Fear not, my lovely angel incarnation
    I will protect you from all wishes of harm
    Including yourself, come praise or damnation."

Angel pet, obviously pulled by his charm
But, for some reason, still in a panicked state
Did she not hear him say no need for alarm?
A good thing our king's decided she's his mate
To deal with it, we wouldn't have the patience
Peasants, are we not right? They tend to frustrate

"But I know what I heard. I felt a presence,"
This vexatious Angel says, shivering quite
    "I was told a tale of woe, of complaisance
    I know not if guide or warning in the night
    A twisted good from a lonely heart of dark
    Father always said nothing is black and white
    Here I feel it the most, how right his remark
    No black *and* white, one swallowing the other
    Swallowing more and more until all's left stark."

Our king sighs, wondering of his odd lover
    "I know not where this inane prattle comes from
    But obviously you need to recover
    Besides, I feel we'll soon be leaving this slum
    You'll need your strength when we go for my last prize
    And the task, when finally we overcome

    I'll do that which I could only dream and fantasize
    Claim my crown and remove any who'd say otherwise."

CHAPTER 16

The morning wakes to a terrible screaming
The Queen! Her cries cutting through the crisp cockcrow
Servants in shroud racing through daylight teeming—
With concern, their other duties they forego
The nobles, last night's guests, join in the pursuit
The relaxed guards now grabbing sword and crossbow
Out of the castle, the gardens they're en route
All converge to where the screams turn to loud wails
To a sight to shock even the strongest brute
Over all, red blood, on their lips prayer fails

The Heir, his sword sunk deep in his father's gut
His face like that of a monster from old tales
Snarling, crazed, vacant, he lifts his sword to cut—
Clean across the throat of the butchered old King
Bathed in crimson, desire for blood he's to glut

Stab again and again, every drop he'll wring
Warm yourself with all that's there! Drink it up, boy
Relish the bliss that only slaughter can bring
But the blood has stopped, and you've skills to employ

Where's the next one? There! Grab her! Sink in your sword!
Shouts all around you, but you've kills to enjoy
There's pain! A crossbow bolt sticks out of you, lord!
Grab her quick! Gut her, slice her, free the inside
Find out how much blood your next victim has stored
Another bolt lands in you, more with each stride
One in the arm, leg, your vision is blurring
But you can't be put down, not before she's died

Then a gasp cuts through the air, pain occurring
It's your own, dear Heir. Do you feel your lungs burn?
Stopped in your tracks by a coldness enduring
Red blind haze pushed from sight, now it's darkness' turn
Steel peeks out your chest from the sword in your back

Wielded by he, past the point of no return
A man of similar face, shaking attack
It's he who robbed you of even your last thoughts
Your mind is unhinged, a sense amnesiac

As the wielder pulls the blade free, you see spots
Never to know why, or realize your death
Just another pawn in a series of plots
Your hearing goes out, you pull in no more breath
You're a shadow now, watching your own demise
Able to bathe in the angels' shibboleth

Thus ends the Heir, surrounded by screams and cries
Quick as it started, now all is hushed silence
Everyone looks to everyone in surprise

The Prince drops the blade, bloodstained with violence
As our king watches from his chamber window
Prime seat to view the sealing of alliance
And watch the retching of the Prince crescendo
As he falls to his knees, unable to stand
In front of his mother, kingdom's new widow

Then summoning unknown strength by will's demand
The Prince pushes to his feet, ready to speak
    "Tragedy has occurred. King dead by son's hand
    A usurpation, desire for havoc to wreak
    Thwarted by my quick thinking, though it pained me
    All saw how he left no choice, sanity bleak
    What could have caused the Heir's such bloodthirsty glee?
    Perhaps the… the sun or destiny too grand!

    But thank God I was here to stop his death spree
    Who knows where next he'd turn? Plague upon the land
    Now only to plague my heart as it shatters
    My relief and despair going hand-in-hand
    Duty compels even when insight scatters
    My brother and father, your heir-prince and king
    My oath to all, not just family matters
    So here I stand, last of that great king's offspring
    And beg your clemency for saving your lives
    By ending my family's." His eyes, tears cling

Where once was terror, now confusion arrives
Our king watches the onlookers, growing throng
His eyes move to the Prince, who hopes he survives

He needs them on his side, opinion is strong
But Frey knows all, and one by one they drop guard
Joining their Prince at his side, bought by his song

The Prince catches our king's gaze across the yard
A silent declaration between the two
As they led away the Queen, memory scarred

And now with eyes forward, the Prince claims his due
His coronation as ruler of the realm
The celebration comes swift for all to view
To behold the passing of the royal helm
As they placed a gold crown on not just one head
But two, a heavenly sight to overwhelm
Hair of ivory, skin of snow, quickly wed
Her diadem with rubies red as her eyes
A serene face where no emotion is shed

The Prince clasps her to his side, knotting their ties
His future now fully under his control
Thanks to helpful advice from certain allies
Allies who now stalk the halls for their own goal
With altruism at an end, no time to stall
Our king, the mastermind, to exact his toll

But on his way, he witnesses a cabal
The Friend, dark shadows under eyes of anguish
With the one who this farce was for, above all
White hair, rose eyes, she who makes men's hearts languish
They are huddled close, want to be out of sight

Foreheads touching, they speak an obscure language
One of subtle expressions and movements slight
Picked up from years in the other's company
A kind hand on her shoulder, then he takes flight
Leaving the woman in quiet custody
Unsure of the questions swimming in her mind
Yet what are her thoughts but a redundancy?

Our king to remind her as he's so inclined
When she stands up to exit her hidden den
Out loud, he speaks, "Marriage contract barely signed
    And already engaging with other men."

The white-haired one raises her stare, unimpressed
Pay no mind to his words, you tragedienne
It's not personal, his plan just can't be messed
Now don't drag this out by trying to defend—
What was seen by your dear husband's honoured guest

But alas, we're ignored and lies she'll extend
    "I see, a question of character, is it?
    If I say I was merely meeting a friend?"

Our king snorts, "Ah yes, you appeared quite close-knit
    But some advice? Be warned of the man's own thought
    Friendship between the sexes is counterfeit
    Especially when just one has tied the knot
    It can make desire stronger than mortal swains
    Before one whose beauty makes decency rot."

She comes to him, so close he can see her veins
Blue rivers beneath her snow white complexion
Trails to follow when on lusty campaigns
Her eyes ensnare his, holding the connection
She asks, "Spoken with familiarity?
    I weep for the women with your affection."

A smirk on him at her tone's austerity
As Wrenfrey responds, "Is that defensiveness?"

But she answers back, "No, it's sincerity
    However, I understand the pensiveness
    When one faces so foreign an expression
    It's why you lack in verbal offensiveness."

Our king witnessing a viper's egression
Ghostly, unearthly, sight to ne'er be unseen
Devil's temptation or angel's accession
His smirk gone. "Quite the one you choose to demean
    After all I did, after all that was done
    You dare to speak to me like that, little queen?"

A tilt of her head, a madonna finespun
    "And what all was done for my happy marriage?
    Will you say? Explain why it made my friend run?"

Wrenfrey's mouth snaps shut. The goal to disparage
Yet he will not budge, for releasing details—
Would be a conversational miscarriage

Her voice low now, in it where resolve assails
    "Speak once again of one's rotting decency
    Hanging off their integrity's short coattails
    So sure of deaf ears and blind eyes frequency
    They accidentally follow the same path
    Deaf and blind to those that see the recency
    Can guess actions taken in their aftermath."
She leans forward, her hand to his bearded chin
    "Oh, Wrenfrey, when will you drown in this bloodbath?"

A shiver runs through him, a jolt from her skin
This feeling, head to toe, surges cold as ice
Cold as life's cruelty, tantalising as sin
This wisp-like touch, her thumb brushes his lip twice
It calls to him with tempting song, tempting fate
Lulling his eyes closed to better hear their vice

He hears nothing else, his breathing nor heart rate
Beckoning him, to molest the void within
Venus flytrap, Lilith's tail wrapping her bait
That's what you are, Wrenfrey, who you've always been

A thousand scars, but that will have to suffice
As before more is had, a voice rushes in
Belonging to one Angel from paradise
    "My lord, my lord, I have come with the new king
    As you requested, he's here to pay your price."

Angel appears with the old Prince following
Grey eyes land on a snow white hand's position

And the room's tension becomes taut as a bowstring
The white-haired one steps back, aiding transition—
To calmer surroundings, Angel relaxes
The Prince speaks, unaware, lacking cognition
    "My promise is as sure as death and taxes
    Let us venture where mortals have never tread
    The two proud kings, tale of the two Ajaxs."

How apt a likeness for our king, born and bred
Travelling to new lands, slaughtering his foes
Before him, all the treasures of seiged Troy spread
We can't wait to see how this story's end goes
And neither can our king as he steps forward
    "Then why're we standing around like we've all froze?
    Like a shipwrecked seafarer swimming shoreward
    Let's move with purpose. Come, my fellow Ajax
    In fact, our women as well, your wife, my ward
    Let's all go to witness this journey's climax
    Might be the only one your new wife receives."
Our king elbows the new king with a laugh lax

But Angel can see where vexation aggrieves
With narrowed eyes, she turns to the white-haired one
Who stares back with crimson, granting no reprieves

The new king clears his throat, no match for our favoured son
    "Come on then, let's all go and get this over and done."

CHAPTER 17

The four of them navigate to the throne room
Behind the thrones, to a door carved in the wall
The new king opens it, entrance like a tomb
Taunting the comers and their astounding gall

"Follow me," the new king says. "To deepest Hell
To empty for the first time, once and for all."

Down a hall, with nerves they could not seem to quell
Our king steps behind his little protégé
His heart beats, eager to reach where treasures dwell
Until at last, it appears, that of dismay
A door of strong old wood, a crest adorning
Snakes, flowers reflect in Angel's eyes of grey
And it's she who speaks, discretion she's scorning
"What's this place? Enigma here, I can't explain
My gut's trepidation I take as warning
Whatever lies beyond, perhaps we abstain
I fear what more could happen should we proceed
I sense only misery, darkness, and pain."

The lowly peasant is a different breed—
From our strapping king, ever closer to we
He who ignores, and drags the new king in greed
To the door he shoves him before he can flee
The now nervous man, limbs barely in control
Our king says, "The deal or the truth I set free."

Proper encouragement gets the ball to roll
The new king places a hand on the wood door
And they all observe as a rot takes its toll
Spreading from the new king's touch, ceiling to floor
Twisting the wood, viscous red leaks from the knot
Until their objective is blocked nevermore
Revealing a chamber, untouched by what rots
Cold, dark, a single chest upon an altar
The new king is afraid, swimming in his thoughts
While our king is solid, Rock of Gibraltar
Pillar of Heracles, a man his rival

   "Well, go on then," our king says. "Let's not falter
   Come now, babe king, no time for fright's revival
   To the task assigned, go get me what is mine
   The chest inside the vault, my good disciple."

The young man is terror-stricken, lacking spine
He wanders a step closer to our Wrenfrey
In whisper, he asks, "What of the curse consigned?
   No further I'll go, on this side I must stay
   I have opened the door. Surely that's enough."
The new king's eyes beg, imploring for leeway

But our king is undeterred, the plea rebuff
    "What happened to calling it ridiculous?
    The only one with sanity. That a bluff?
    If not, then you find one who's meticulous—
    For doing as they're told, and it'd best be now
    I care not to deal with one who's mischievous
    Perhaps your bride? Yes, your bride I will allow
    Send her in to combat what your sane mind fears
    Either you or her, decide the who and how."

The new king's face is red, on the verge of tears
Pathetic display, so easy to coerce
It's doubtful the two kings would ever be peers
At least between him and her, he knows the verse
Value yourself. You're the only one who will
Ne'er sacrifice for others, that's the true curse

At last the babe king speaks up, his voice quite shrill
    "My love, I've a task which needs your assistance
    For my friend here, I've a promise to fulfil."

The white-haired one and Angel cross the distance
Her musical tone comes next, "What must I do?"

Her husband now, "He asks with some insistence
    For the box just beyond. Let this not fall through
    It is a simple undertaking, really
    And then you can leave this foul place behind you."

Her eyes scorch him, oppressive this fair lily
To anyone of lesser stock, it would scare
But our great king smirks at the frilled up filly
Wrenfrey claps his hands. "Come now, girl, time to share
    We've pulled our weight through these toilings, you pull yours
    Fetch the darkened box so we can be elsewhere."

The white-haired one, where the new king's courage stores
Her face empty, clasps the hand of our king's girl
    "Very well. She will come as I do your chores
    For I am sure no objection you will hurl
    As safety is, no doubt, always on your mind
    All subjects equal, whether loved one or churl."

Angel's nervousness he wishes to unwind
Her protection in all things our king is sworn
But he remains strong. She understands his bind
He can't let this woman think she's higher born

So he steps aside, gesturing them onward
The white-haired one and Angel pass, left forlorn
Grey eyes find his for a split second, his ward
'Fore they turn away, follow the gaze of red
The new king's hand is on the hilt of his sword
White knuckles on the pommel, heart filled with dread
Our king, so generous with his time, assists
Take mind off what honour babe king's left to shed

    "A warning before and my warning persists,"
Wrenfrey says, "Careful with her, she'll eat you whole

Liable to run off when weakness exists
To some other royalty, stronger and droll
Women are wild creatures, in need of taming
You're the man, so assume your ancestral role
I say this to spare your pride further maiming
From what I saw following coronation
It seems prudent for the future you're framing

Who knows if your queen is queen of this nation
And not a *certain neighbour* of weak morals
Averse to help your ascension's formation."

The new king is angry, ready for quarrels
Lost his sense at the thought our king has proposed
    "The cur wouldn't dare try to steal my laurels!"

Our king speaks, "More will try, if left unopposed
    Not just for your wife but for crown and birthright
    Place all under heel, your will to be imposed
    You are the king, every day will be a fight
    Against those who wish to steal your rightful throne
    Advice I've lived my life by each day and night

    There is no one your equal, you are alone
    God's chosen, thus entitled to all and more
    Ne'er forget, all's yours, twig and stone, blood and bone."

His words strike a chord, the new king's mind at war
Still so when the women return, box in hand
Wrenfrey, expectant for the prize he sent for

Who says, "I wish to see inside, what's so grand—
     To be locked in a cursed vault, cause such a fuss
     Open it please, so we may all understand."

Their interest raised, so no need to discuss
Her pale hands lift the lid to reveal inside—
That this box is… less interesting to us

Bones lay here, tiny, ivory, free of hide
Skull in odd pieces, but a human's no doubt
Muscle and viscera pulled free when it died

     "A crypt all this time, the job we held devout."
The new king speaks, "Naught but wardens of the dead."

Angel comes to our king, quiet words squeak out
     "Don't, please." But he's not done pulling on this thread

He speaks, "Relax, my Angel, we're past halfway
     One task more and a traitor I will behead."

He relieves the box from the pale woman's sway
The clatter and chatter of bones trapped within
Satisfied at last he bids the two good-day,
     "My lady, an honour. Our meeting a win
     To the babe king, remember what I told you
     And I'm sure one day you'll rise to be my twin."

And off they went, with one last prize to accrue
Stepping from the throne room into the courtyard

Deathly quiet, no movement from those in view
The servants are still, their shrouds act as a guard—
Against judgement, for them and those their eyes stalk
Still, their veiled gaze is an oppressive bombard

Scorching Angel pet, the expressionless mock
Our king's oblivious or just uncaring
As they make their way past ghosts who like to gawk
Their presence exacting, their silence blaring
Angel can hardly breathe when they make the gate
Need to be free of their eternal staring

She gives the castle one last look, left too late
This feeling of failure welling up inside
Need to understand, recognition to sate

Nurture those feelings, Angel pet, them to guide
As your eyes spy someone on the rampart's end
A royal wife whose mind has already died
She wills her body to follow, sense suspend
Feet attempt to continue their walk on air
As the poor Queen falls so that she might ascend
Trailing above is her endless golden hair
A lifeline attached to nothing. It runs out
Closer and closer, the hard ground wants to share
Angel's frozen, stuck in her throat is her shout
What she sees… her thoughts can't process, won't process
Closer and closer, the impact's just about…

The gate shuts on her view of a life's egress
The sight not to be branded upon her mind
Just the sound, a strangely soft thud spells success

She stands there unmoving, like a guard assigned
Until our king moves her along, unaware
He who only looks forward, never behind
His strides confident while hers are without care
Let's not waste time, Angel, let's pick up the pace
Move along. Our patience is starting to wear
Dragging this out won't make destiny erase
Denying us only results in encore
No change but the amount of egg on your face

Now enough of that, the Hand greets you once more
The five goliaths gazing down at our king
To observe the box from their revered queen's chore
Titan, the leader, ever the brutish thing
He doesn't acknowledge the brilliance of our lord
Such is life, when ignorance is so wellspring
Titan says, "Longer this time, for your reward
    Was it hesitation, qualms, a change of heart?
    Did you let someone get where your thoughts are stored?"

Our king brushes away all from this upstart
Ignorance *and* lunacy are on the rise
He speaks, "Nothing keeps me and my crown apart
    Let it be witnessed in my future war cries
    All who try will be brought before my mercy
    And only to find I have none to reprise

Call me a deceiver, a son of Circe
But I will return to my place of power
And know it won't come without controversy."

Poor Angel pet hears these words, dark and dour
They breed with what happened mere moments before
A deep darkness that leaves her soul to cower
An ocean that crashes her upon the shore

Yet she can't escape as it pulls her back here
To be battered again, so she'll ask for more
A hand on her shoulder, Titan's shroud veneer
    "Let us be off, little flower. Shan't be long—
    'Fore we see our Majesty, the goal made clear
    Pray, why do you look so? Like you don't belong?
    Your mind's a wonderfully terrible trap
    For every good thought, bad ones come as a throng

    You know you can end this quick as fingers snap
    You need to wake up to them and what they spawn
    Do not hide from them. Find the source, close the gap

    You can do it this time with the lines you've drawn
    You must realize what's happening happened
    Only then can we all finally move on."

Angel's brows pull together, Titan maddened
Poor her, not understanding this sudden speech
Our king to the rescue. "I'm sure you're gladdened—
    To help, my good man, but don't dare overreach

Scare ladies with nonsense, you'll drive them away
Scare *my* lady and there's a lesson to teach
Now let us move, your queen hasn't got all day
And I'd very much like to be gone from here
For each second, foul Krios leads more astray."

Titan and his men, the Hand, step back in fear—
Of our great king's threat, years are knocked off their lives
As Titan gives a final look, one to sear
They lead them back to where dark magic survives
Passing by a familiar spot, one well-known
A place where Angel's uncertainty derives

The bodies are gone, but memories are carved in bone
None see the willows reach or hear the crying wind blown

CHAPTER 18

Back to purgatory's home away from home
Once more they find themselves in royalty's halls
Amongst decorations that fill catacombs
The walls now embellished with swords, shields, and mauls
Our king catches Angel's hand, her heart alight
He says, "Take care ever that horseman's pick falls
    Not good to be under unless you're a knight
    With a proper helmet forged of strongest steel
    And even then you may kiss yourself goodnight."

A small smile on Angel's lips, one kiss to steal
Elation his expression, he points out more
    "And this flail, worst invention for war's ordeal
    Idiots swing them 'round, like heroes from lore
    But knock themselves out before battle's begun
    Around the shield they teach, to find hands to gore
    But easier to teach cats water is fun
    Want to destroy your enemy? Give them flails."

Angel is laughing, his passion overrun
Showcasing weapons, armour, and their details

Different shapes and sizes, brutal and graceful
As they walk our king brings to life each one's tales
Her face is constant smiles, his task successful
He pulls her in close, wanting to clear the air
Our king speaks, "My Angel, for you I'm grateful

    Light in the darkness of this sordid affair
    But in the actions I've taken here and then
    I am sorry if you've been caused quite a scare
    My destiny, moved by forces beyond ken
    They act through me to ensure my victory
    And all deeds that I do I would do again
    My crown I must reclaim, rewrite history
    Foul Krios defeated for the good of all

    So I deal with this queen and her witchery
    Act her will that would cause lesser men to fall
    To safeguard you and our future together
    And to salvage my dignity overall
    Now that I've put you at ease, no more blether
    The queen of shadows awaits my appearance
    And I dare not spend too long in this aether."

The servants are there allowing their clearance
Through the gut-wrenching door of flower and snake
To a figure that tests mind's perseverance
A bundle of cloth resting at the throne's wake
The still pulsating organs resting on top
Never to give sensibilities a break

The queen doesn't move when the two come to a stop
Patient, waiting for our king to say his piece
He does so, stepping up, ready to talk shop
    "My beautiful queen! Let your heart be at peace
    For we return with the object you require
    Proven my intellect with a simple fleece
    'Twas your enemy's not a moment prior
    But now you may behold the chest, what's inside
    I'm ready for the next object to acquire
    Though surely now you see with who you've allied
    Must we stick with these trials? Let's end this dance
    I know our energies are better applied."

But no answer comes from across the expanse
No agreement to such a sound suggestion
Instead she calls her champion with a glance
Titan steps forth, "It was done without question
    A new foundation laid for decades to come
    The old done, removed archaic congestion
    The king brought the dominion under his thumb
    To achieve his ends he let none in his way—
    Escape unscathed, all who'd threaten his kingdom."

Words from one she trusts, her silence ends its stay
A throat of gargling glass shards is the voice
Ne'er to be accustomed to, makes ears fillet
    "Produce the chest, fallen king, I should rejoice
    Taken from the depths, the kingdom's very heart
    Skillfully retrieved from a prince with no choice."

More sure this time, eagerness his counterpart
He lifts the chest before the queen, lid open
The tiny bones on display, ivory art

Bear witness to the queen's dress, like an omen
The trailing hem, smoky, slinks down her throne stairs
Slithering on the ground towards the token

It stops before him, black hole beyond prayers
No creases of fabric, just infinite void
A void that stares back as reality tears

"Empty it."

He does so, careful movement, not too annoyed—
To be ordered by someone below his rank
Not sure this creature is even humanoid
But he was God's chosen, it's His strength we thank
To give our god the fortitude to stand firm
With such evil flaunting with audacious swank

The bones are caught, brought to the organs that squirm
The dark nothingness settles over them both
With a solemn quiet that's carried to term
Only broken by our king and his regrowth—
Of confidence, ready to get on with it
    "If immediate partnership with my troth
    Alludes your wisdom still, say where next to flit
    And I'll be off to prove on this final task

The worthiness of your men under my wit
Where next do you send this pilgrimage? I ask
What next am I to take to demonstrate skill?
Who next to bathe in my presence as your mask?"
Severe as ice, swirling frost makes the room chill
Stronger, intense, more than they suffered before
The Majesty's voice comes, abhorrent and shrill
    "It is thus: memory comes for an encore
    What you're to seek lies with the Twin of the Friend
    Her most prized possession, and an inner war
    Try as she might it's something she must pretend—
    Does not exist for fear of the whole world's wrath
    So she'll hide it 'til the day she's to ascend

    Your task to retrieve it, but free from bloodbath
    For just one misstep and it's locked forever
    A delicate tight-rope, seduction your path
    For she will not give it, unless you're clever
    Convince her your destinies are intertwined
    Then take what she has, merciless as ever

    Beware her brother, an obstacle you'll find
    Still guarded from the happenings with the Prince
    He's a protective man with an axe to grind."

Two emotions, the first makes Angel pet wince
For obvious reasons her fear's evident
Her poor heart, this new task will turn it to mince

The second makes our king a true celebrant
A more perfect mission he couldn't wish for
With this the man's victory was definite
But he maintains the humbleness all adore
Tempered are his next words, "If this is what's asked
    I'll do what I must as the powers implore."

And *who* he must, our cheeky king thinks, glee vast
A demonstration of his true talents plied
To do something worthy of him at long last
But the face framed in crimson locks at his side
Does he not see or willfully ignoring?

The queen resumes, "Go, fallen king, true and tried
    And on your return we'll get to some warring
    Unless, of course, you feel desire's diminished
    To give up your crown, forget the restoring
    Realize your past faults, old pride relinquished
    Come to terms with the happenings around you
    Say this, fallen king, and we will be finished."

Angel's hopeful, her insides twisted askew
She goes to take his hand but 'fore she can grasp—
Our king steps closer to the throne, "I'll be through—
    When, with my help, Krios takes his final gasp
    His blood to feed the trees, his body the crows
    I'll be through when my crown and birthright I clasp
    Not a moment sooner than Krios' death throes
    Have no fear, dear queen, I'll not abandon this

There's no indecision in me to expose
Especially not over some woman's kiss
I'll stay this course, I've seen my future's brightness
To deviate I would surely be remiss."

The queen, she appreciates his forthrightness
We tell by her shoulders falling, tension lost
Her voice comes with the usual politeness,
    "You'll be the Twin's dearest flame, despite the cost
    You'll understand what that title underscores
    You'll know the moment when words and speech exhaust

    But should you go astray, return on all fours
    Beg my forgiveness, implore my acceptance
    Let the mortification seep from your pores

    Plead your sin before us all, show us your repentance
    And we will listen and debate our acquiescence."

CHAPTER 19

Angel walks along the path beside our king
The group on their way to seduce some woman
She didn't expect such eagerness, the sting
She's not to be sad, it's just part of the plan
But it still hurts. They should leave this all behind

But he won't. He said as much when this began
Was there anything to do? Loopholes to find?
A feeling of dread was lazily creeping
Seeping from the blood on this contract he signed

As she walks next to our king, inner weepings
Joined by Titan, obscured face and intention
He speaks through his veil, "This way to their keepings
   But heed my warning, the lands fill with tension
   Relations strained between the Prince and the Friend
   And your coming won't aid its circumvention
   Our queen sends you on a mission of pretend
   Sent to rebuild diplomacy, this your guise
   The Friend wants nothing more than friendship to mend

But how can it, after what he saw arise?
The Friend knows what was done by the Prince, by you
It'll be hard to convince the man otherwise."

Our king huffs, "Who cares about his point of view?
He's a boy always stuck in others' shadows
The Friend had his chance for favour to accrue
He's just mad that when things became hard, he froze
And I reaped the benefits his absence brought
Perhaps he'll learn there are those you don't oppose
When I leave his dearest sister, sadness wrought."

Titan is emotionless, his voice empty
"As you say, Highness, worry no afterthought
We do not judge, our job to watch is plenty
To witness whatever decisions you make
And report all things important and petty
But a storm is approaching across the lake
Best to take shelter, a near cabin to use
And the Hand shall see what you leave in your wake."

Whirling and twirling, a demon on the loose
It's the only explanation for the sky
Wanting to rip the trees, every oak and spruce
The storm comes faster than Titan's words imply
He and his brothers melding with the darkness
Out of sight amongst the rain, to watch and spy
Our king pulls Angel close, for he's not heartless
The torrenting rain comes in sheets as they run
Quick, 'fore one of them ends up a drowned carcass

There! The cabin! In the door! Outside they shun
They brush off the water, drenched from head to toe
Only our great king's smile adds light where there's none
　　"More warning next time. He was a little slow,"
Our king says with a laugh, shaking out his hair
　　"Unless, of course, this look makes your heart aglow."

Angel smiles despite herself. He's just not fair
As she squeezes out her dress, he makes a fire
Down in the wood cabin's hearth for the drenched pair
Flickering flame dances to an unheard lyre
Angel enjoys the heat, feeling much better
And our lusty king's predicament grows dire

Wet cloth clinging to her form, a love letter
One he must examine meticulously
Swelling chest, ruby cheeks, all the abettor

But instead Angel speaks ridiculously
　　"Do you mean what you said, talking to Titan?
　　I care not for you speaking so viciously
　　Leaving her wrought from sadness, it does frighten
　　Do you intend to leave all in such a way?"

Ah, there's that concern he does so delight in
Watching her squirm under his gaze like his prey
Our mouths water for the scraps our king will leave

He closes in, her in his arms, eyes of grey
　　"My lovely Angel, I beg you not to grieve

I say only what makes me seem resolute
Must be strong for the queen's men 'lest they perceive—
Me as soft or unworthy to persecute—
My foes when I take the reins as their master
As for the woman whose heart I'm to uproot
God knows, I wish not to cause a disaster
If only there was another way, alas
I hope she'll be able to put it past her."

Angel is ecstatic, wrapped up in his mass
To him, she says, "But there is another way
Leave with me, become one of the lower class
Your honour intact, you step out of the fray
No longer held in chains of retribution
Instead, free with me to go about our day."

Annoyance full force for her 'resolution'
His jaw clicks, a sigh builds up inside his chest
He's ready to end this with absolution

But lo! The wood door swings open! A new guest!
A woman hidden in cloak, soaked from the rain
It's she! The Friend's Twin! Quick, you must look your best!
A push and Angel is out of his arms' strain
Free to tumble back as the Twin's brown eyes lift
A look of shock but a tickle in her brain
A gasp, she speaks, "Why, it's you! Night's sudden shift
Where did you come from? What are you doing here?
Especially when there still remains a rift—
That raises ire when brought to my brother's ear

Between the two kingdoms, though, I know not why
It's all caused quite a scandalous atmosphere."

But our king is quick, and ready with words sly
A chuckle and practiced smile upon his lips
    "What am I doing here? The same I'll apply—
    To a certain woman taking moonlit trips
    A dark night's unsafe for one so beautiful
    All matter of thugs, wolves, with you in their grips
    Pray tell, troubles at home stir the dutiful?
    Send you running for fear of suffocation?
    Do you search for somewhere that's more suitable?"

The Twin gasps. A psychic is his vocation
    "It's exactly as you say. How could you tell?
    Years I'm smothered by my brother's protection
    And I wish to be free of it, him as well
    To see who I want, to... to love who I want
    I'm an adult and I wish out of this hell."
The Twin crosses her arms, drunk from courage's font

Our king wanders near, a hand to her wet head—
Twirls wet hair. "And how goes your new life's first jaunt?"

His sudden closeness, she barely hears what's said
Her hands twisting around her cloak's dampened hem
As she gulps, her face turning a crimson red
    "I didn't expect such turbulent mayhem—
    To pour from the skies or force me to this hut
    But now I wonder if it's fate's hidden gem

To find such fineness, who am I to rebut?
I still can't believe you're here, feels like ages—
Since I last saw you, before borders were shut."

Our king nods, the first in his plan of stages
"Takes quality to recognize quality
But know the beast of diplomacy rages
Your brother, I wish to mend the jollity—
Between the nations and between us two men
I dare hope a return to equality."

She is elated. "It's wonderful news, then!
I desire nothing more than what you've just said
Let's return together. A treaty to pen
The rain has stopped, the castle's not far ahead
A mere hour's ride is all I could muster—
Before the storm forced me to this tiny shed."

Joy in her eyes. Our king knows he can trust her
She pulls back from him and exits the cabin
Her absence leaving the whole place lacklustre
She's like food to a man after a famine
Empty all his life 'til that very moment
He feels more alive than he can imagine

Then there's a faint cough, the corner's bestowment
A redheaded peasant awkwardly standing
Wide grey eyes of his forgotten component

Our king asks, "Angel, am I not outstanding?
    Already I can see the lust in her eyes
    Simple touch sparks it, it's mine for commanding
    Perhaps a single night to get the queen's prize
    And we can soon return, back to my homeland
    All I need do is remember all my lies."

He ends with a laugh, simple comment offhand
Following out after his shiny new toy
Leaving behind Angel, the dimming firebrand—
To catch up with the two and the twisted ploy
A chill heavy in her stomach weighs her down
To move took all the effort she could employ
As outside the cabin, not a single frown
The Twin rests on her horse with our king by her
Moonlight on her raven hair and eyes of brown
Eyes of brown that find eyes of grey, both minds stir

But our great king brushes away any fears
    "My servant, princess. No trouble, I assure
    Helpful here and there as I scale the frontiers
    Fine company to talk to on those long treks
    But I'm happy now to be amongst my peers
    Shall we journey to see brother and subjects?
    We'll return 'fore they even knew you were gone
    And I'll get to work on a job so complex."

The Twin nods, a smile beautiful as the dawn
As the three wander down the empty dirt street
Unknown to the torment this short walk will spawn

Soon at the castle, it is panic they greet
Torches ablaze, the guard in hysteria
Woman's emotion grips them from head to feet
Ordered by their king to fan the area
The grounds to be combed, the forests to be searched
To be no sleep until the next feria!

But a keen eye spots a horse, a rider perched
Two walk at its sides, one of elegant make
And the other one of peasant-birth, besmirched

The rider drops her hood in the searchers' wake
Alarms sound, the trio's beset by the guard
Familiar shrouds on their heads, each tailor-make

The Friend appears, vicious gaze on our vanguard
    "What's the meaning of this?" His voice, careful rage
Traditional pleasantries the men discard

    "Dear brother, put your anger back in its cage,"
The Twin speaks, "I merely went for a night's ride
    Bumped into an old friend, no need for rampage
    He's here with my blessing and comes to confide
    Listen to him, talks of peace between kingdoms
    He's come so far, I won't let him be denied."

The Friend hot, the grinding of teeth, his victims
To deny our king is to risk besmirchment

When one goes contrary to higher wisdoms
    "Then to your room, sister, I'll hold my judgement,"
He says, "I'll see to the guest, much to discuss
    Though I believe what's said will be redundant."

Whisked through the halls, gaudy and superfluous
The Twin escorted away to her bedroom
The Friend escorts our king, whose strength is with us

In a chamber they stop, the Friend to resume—
His growing anger at his home's parasite
    "You killed the King and his Heir, you were their doom
    Unknown method, but I heard your words that night
    Words of a madman, teetering sanity
    And now here you come, for history's rewrite."

Our king is unfazed by this profanity
To it, he says, "Yet none know but you and I
    Why, I wonder, to protect your vanity?
    No help for a friend, choosing instead to cry
    And entangle fingers in certain white locks
    Bizarre behaviour for one's only ally."

The Friend stands silent, words stuck in his voice box
So our king continues, "But that's in the past
    I wish for friendship, not this thing stained with pox
    Let us speak of peace, of something that will last
    I'll prove my commitment to you if need be
    I wish not the role of 'friend' to be recast."

Spark of hope in the Friend's eye tries to break free
But tamped down by reasonable suspicion
    "And my soul the next you make an absentee?"

Our king's lips thin, tired of this dull audition
He turns to leave, over his shoulder he tells,
    "You're lucky it's me and not a physician
    She was not on a stroll, but ringing Death's bells
    Your sister was leaving you. I turned her back
    Know that before enmity further compels."

To the hall, Angel's surprised at this setback
They stomp to the front door, pressed as well, to leave
Hand to pull open but a shout makes it slack

The Friend catches them, desperate to believe
    "One month!" He says. "Ready negotiation
    Best not make me regret with plans to deceive
    Or for every one soldier in your nation
    A hundred of mine will march without mercy

    Oh, and my sister equals your castration."

Our king holds up his hands. "No controversy—
    To be found here. All I want is to progress
    Move forward and not end things too adversely."

The Friend, a room and an ear he'll acquiesce
    "And for your companion?" he asks of our king

Who shrugs it off, "Little concern, I confess
    With her kin, other servants under your wing
    I'll fetch her on my journey back. Until then—
    Let's reconvene in the morn, weigh everything
    I've one month, I'll prove myself time and again
    For both our sakes, let our reunion shed hate
    Let us rise stronger as not just friends, but men."

    "You always were the charismatic ingrate,"
The Friend says while our king turns to his peon
A wink to her, a wink she cannot translate

    "Wrenfrey?" Angel asks, her soft voice plebeian
Guards arrive at her side to take her away
We can hardly wait to sing our king's paean

Crimson hair from a sliding memory led astray
As the next stage in a long list is about to play

CHAPTER 20

What can we say about our erudite king
That has not already been proclaimed tenfold
By all who have been taken under his wing?
A man of tactics, brains, a prophet foretold
A man to show other men how it's all done
And to outshine even the most polished gold

As we're nearing the end of the first week's run
Our king delights without gaining suspicion
The Friend relaxes, unraveling doubt spun
The warm comfort of nostalgia the mission
Each day, the Friend's shoulders loosen ever so
More and more peace, less and less inhibition

Days spent in memories of summer and snow
The Friend prattles on about long gone childhood
Two princes and a white-haired girl who forego—
Morning lessons to protect the common good
With swords, they fight invisible troglodytes
With shields, they defend against their adulthood

But still it came. They gave simpler times last rites
In the tangled ball of Mettle and Cunning
Came their shadows of Abuse and Careful Slights
Trying to hold to memories they're shunning
'Fore complex became a synonym for life
Trying to hold water that's overrunning

Yet now an extra pair of hands help the strife
The wrinkles on the man's brow have receded
A smile returns, twinkling eyes, laughter rife
Talks of negotiations superseded
To talk about the time the Friend and his friend—
Were lost in the forest, their nerves exceeded
The white-haired girl then appearing on the bend
She could get them out, but on one condition
Her slaves for the day, her whims they were to tend
Unease growing, they'd suffer the affliction
Let it be known the white-haired girl kept her word

A single branch moved completed her mission
The castle not a stone's throw away! Absurd!
Embarrassing! Turned around in the backyard!
And so the two boys trudged back with their smug third

The Friend took the brunt of their promise, left scarred
By the dresses she made him wear, frills and pomp
But she smiled, so he could handle his pride marred
The other boy was smart, he escaped the romp
Leaving his Friend to her mercy as he hid
Even though later it earned him the girl's whomp

Such are the things discussed, memoirs of a kid
Between ales and wines, conversation stretching
Before darkness catches and goodnights are bid
Then our king makes his way to true goal's fetching

Captivating his mark with practiced routine
But don't mistake his ways as common leching
The thrill is the chase, each setback and careen
Overcome, overpower, he's an artist
And when has real art ever been quick and clean?

It is chaotic even for the smartest
True strength lies in adaption and right moments
Lest away the opportunity is pissed

And our king has been busy with all segments
Not a point in time his prey doesn't feel his gaze
Redness flooding her cheeks with lustful torments
He speaks with cheeky diction and turn-of-phrase
Smiles to melt the heart, with laughs to pull its strings
Sometimes there's an 'accidental' touch or graze
Brush up 'gainst the other in the castle's wings

All this done out of sight of the Friend, of course
If the plan was to move forth without sword swings
Subtle interest he's to drop, then enforce
With every action, make her mind race, heart beat
Catching her hand or helping her on her horse

With every meeting, make resistance deplete
Her throat dry as you brush hair behind her ear
Your thumb stroking her lower lip with smile sweet
With every word, make her precautions unclear
Have her hang on every single syllable
Needed escape from her surroundings austere

Desire for passion, easily tillable
Building and building, and building even more
Between the two, certainty unkillable
Inevitability upon the shore
Where their psyches and judiciousness divorce
And our king leaves with them begging for encore

Now, presently, our king proves himself a force
Before the lake he stands, moonlight upon him
A certain bedroom window a distant source
The occupant inside desire's synonym
He can feel her watching, her bated breath caught
As crystal clear water beckons him to swim

So he shrugs off his cloth, unties belt and knot
His tunic cast aside, silk gracing the ground
Trousers next, removal slow with teasing thought

Then, at last, they're discarded to his clothes mound
Himself free, his body under silver flare
Luminous, each roped muscle blessedly found
Like one of his Greek gods, mortals to beware
As Elysian splendours rest in his looks

And Elysian pleasures rest in his stare
The hearts and minds of the fairer sex he rooks
And to try as one might, one's ability—
To resist like cavalry versus billhooks

He dives into the lake with tranquillity
Each stroke's motion demonstrating his power
As he awaits a hold out's futility
His quarry in the safety of her tower
Heart beating as everything comes to a head
The next catch for lust and longing to devour
Night lighting his body, the sight to embed
Confidence in each kick and push, thrust and twist
A natural gift of this noble purebred

Oh, what this does to us, how can we resist?
Yet we must, this show isn't for our greedy eyes
But the one who now finds herself in our midst

Our watchful king knows, hardly stealthy his prize
He rises from the water like Poseidon
His dignity the same as subtlety dies
A hand he lifts to the wood voyeurs hide in
Gesturing to shades, commanding they appear
As distances between urge and sense widen

He's answered, as out steps a sight to revere
The Twin, naked as he, like a sacrifice
Before the one who would ravage her mind clear

She comes to him, her evermore as the price
Hands run over the moonlit drops on his chest
Fingers trace each ridge of promised paradise
Their stares never leave the other, need confessed
She leans in, breaths now mingling together
He can feel her thudding heart from in her breast
Her lips to his, delicate as a feather
As though thoughts disbelieving of what eyes see
And good sense still holding on by a tether

Now he encases her, sets that good sense free
If Father God's to damn them, then let Him damn
He meets her, joining her with silent decree
Pulling her in, hands upon this little lamb
Passion flaring, overriding heart and soul
And she is as lost as the sons of Priam

Tears fill her eyes as he lays her on the knoll
Dreams of this moment, to the real world they clawed
The two embrace, forgetting the other's role
Now just a man and woman, nymph and her god
As raw heat turns glistening droplets to steam
Giving to the other, their perfect and flawed
Away from obligation's unending stream

Begging pleas, moans, and grunts in the other's ear
Cries swallowed in deep kisses, drowning each scream
These creatures of higher thought we so revere
Their finer minds now focused on just one thing

An end before completion their only fear
Strong building intensity, both a coiled spring
Upon the grass, pleasure filling their bloodstreams
Their minds blanking in the throes as passions wring

And as we watch the two bodies under the moonbeams
We wait for the continuance of consistent themes

CHAPTER 21

And so the week ends, and the new one begins
Until that one follows suit, as does the next
On the fourth now, enjoying infinite sins
Revelling in his plan and every aspect
Purposefully prolonging his gainful stay?
Or taking his time to ensure full effect?

Meh, who are we, the lowly servants, to say?
The wait merely intensifies the relief
When our king at last greets us on full display

But perhaps our saviour hears our silent grief
As he returns to his arrowed path's fletching
To fetch his box from his little love-struck lief
This night he rids himself of the Friend's retching
To wander amongst the castle's large gardens
'Fore a certain window of one so fetching
Not long until he hears a step and hardens
A giggle comes soon after, arms 'round his waist
      "Did I disturb you, sir? A thousand pardons."

The Twin, a delight in a dress barely laced
Yearning in her eyes as desire paints her face
No longer the shadow with affections chaste
Now they meet, hidden, sharing the flowers' space
Sometimes ducking to the gardeners' closet
Sometimes right on the grass, thirsty to debase
Tonight's such a night, one look and that was it
Wrenfrey holds her close, their nightly deed complete
Amongst nature, their nude bodies apposite

Our king's voice is soothing, his soft whispers sweet:
    "How lucky I am, lying with one so fine
    Holy God on our side when he let us meet
    But I worry for the woman I've made mine
    Of highest noble birth yet rutting on dirt
    You deserve more than amongst the weed and vine
    Let us join in your room, if I may be curt
    So I can meet you in a more honest way
    More like a lover and less like a pervert."

She chuckles, then her brows draw with words to weigh
    "I know, but what if my brother were to knock?
    I know what he said to you, about your stay
    Refrain from me or else lose your precious cock."

Our king lifts her delicate chin. "Just my balls,
    I'd still have that little thing which makes you squawk."

    "Squawk?!" She gasps. "Little thing indeed, like a doll's."

They laugh, but our king is serious once more
    "Do you believe he doesn't know his own home's halls—
    Or their happenings? Intellect to his core
    Perception to match. Pick it up when we speak
    Unspoken understanding in our rapport
    He plays blind. Your happiness is yours to seek
    No issue with our union, if out of sight
    And you must agree, outside's lost its mystique."

She bites her lip, concern at war with delight
A want to believe it's as our king reports
But turmoil and fluster keeps worry alight
Our king sighs, pulls away from the one he courts
    "Never mind, wrong of me to want any more
    And I should be off anyway," he retorts

He stands up, and his lover's voice does restore
    "Wait, please, perhaps it is as you say. I hope
    Still, we must be careful to get to my door."

With that, the noose tightens. Our king holds the rope
The breath in his chest, he's sweating the release
Straining against fibers with the hands that grope

But right now, our duo makes it in one piece
The creak of her door the only evidence
Then in the other's arms, this lusty caprice
Once done taking in this lap of decadence
Our keen king spots something of great interest
That sigil to afford him his recompense

The vanity is where it lies, that small chest
Snakes encircling a flower, the queen's mark
Our king's tortuous wait is finally blessed
    "A beautiful box," our king makes his remark,
    "With craftsmanship unlike anything I've seen
    It's fitting for the sister of a monarch
    And inside? I wish more than a shake can glean
    Is it priceless jewels? Or a secret journal?
    Come, open it, and bring light to the unseen."

She grabs her box, is practically maternal
So careful with it, checking over its shape
But only allows looks at the external
She speaks, "Some things I'm not ready to undrape
    Especially to you. Please take no offense
    It's precious as jewels but fragile as a grape

    Perhaps later, when everything's less intense
    I feel it won't be much longer you'll need wait
    Promise not to leave you in too much suspense."

She curls her arms around him, desires to sate
But his desires first as he unwraps from her,
    "But now you've caught my attention with this bait."
He asks, "Maybe just a small peek can occur?
    How else am I to stay enraptured by you
    When you've laid out such an intriguing mind's stir?"

His lover giggles. "I suppose you'll make do
    I'm right here if you wish to fondle a chest

And promise my insides are more your purview."

Our king lets out a heavy sigh, not impressed
His patience is thinning, near a month he's spent
He's done what needs doing. What else to invest?
    "Of course, my forever," he says, fake content
A quick kiss. "We'll pick this up another time
    Until then, in my mind, your face will frequent."

He leaves them wanting, mystery's paradigm
Our glorious king can't see her confusion
Blinded by his own glow, this man in his prime

He exits the room, leaving the seclusion
His plan going according to each part's stage
A bit more and he can drop this illusion
From the book of subterfuge, he's torn a page
A king after our hearts and us after his
This man with the mind of an all-knowing sage
And look at his glee, like a kid whose aced his quiz

Let him live in his moment of dilettante
Not the best time to point out flaws, though when is?
A swagger as he leaves is his little vaunt
No one's watching, only us you must assuage
Each movement of his, each performance, a taunt

His satisfaction building from his silent rampage
He's completely blind to the slowly descending cage

CHAPTER 22

"Two languages she speaks," the Friend says in awe
He's joined by our king in the castle courtyard
Enjoying the warm sun, a day without flaw
The Friend continues on, ever the blowhard
    "The woman I've married is quite a wonder
    Comforting, with a wit to catch you off guard
    I have to think if the whole thing's a blunder
    How could I get someone like her, one so good?
    One look and I swear my heart's torn asunder."

Our king's knowing eyes roll, as only his could
He almost feels bad for the poor man. Almost
When it's obvious he's speaking some falsehood
Our wise king remembers his previous post
And time only assists to make things clearer

The Friend and woman of white hair so engrossed
Their faces close, and only drawing nearer
His hand crawling up her thigh, her arm, her cheek
In their eyes, each other's desires they mirror
Unaware our king was watching the two sneak—

Behind the back of their alleged best friend
Now the Friend lies, but our king knows the technique

Our king asks, "So where's this woman to commend—
    For the taming of such a ferocious beast?
    It's been weeks. Let us meet before the world's end."

The Friend chuckles, not suspecting in the least—
That our great king is always two steps ahead
The Friend answers, "Her father is near deceased
    She's ventured back home to be by his deathbed
    I know not when she'll return, hopefully soon
    Bad to say because it means her father's dead
    But I miss her. I doubt even you're immune
    To sadness felt by the absence of your wife
    A feeling shared, I think, when both are in tune."

Our king nods along. "A cruel twist of the knife
    When your woman leaves you for another man
    Careful, mayhaps she'll stay, resume her old life."

The Friend's eyes narrow, wonder across their span
    "Let's speak about you. Ages since last we talked
    Not met since the closure of borders began
    Then bursting through my doors, I find myself shocked
    These days like reenactments of times of old
    Soon we'll find wood swords and a witch to decoct."

But before our king can spin his words of gold
A servant comes to them, a bow to her lord

"Apologies, there's a matter, I was told
That requires your attention, upon the sward
It seems one of your horses has gotten loose
All attempts to contain him he has ignored
Your ways the stable hands tried to reproduce
But to no avail, and they ask for your aid
Sorry to drag their king in. There's no excuse."

The Friend blinks, then laughs and nods to the young maid
He speaks, "Tell them to fear not. I'm on my way
We'll talk later, my friend, my boy must be swayed."

Off they go, leaving our king to seethe the day
The Friend... playing the false uxorious cad
Nothing but masculinity in decay

Unlike our Wrenfrey, whose own is ironclad
Memories of his past, his noble childhood
Servants would quake at the mere sight of the lad
There was only one soul who misunderstood
The dynamic he crafted since he was born
Challenging our king in ways only she could
She who would steal his love, a story timeworn
Closer they grew, their hearts filling the other's
Each day spent together, into night, then morn

Him with his tales of Zeus and the god's lovers
Her with her unending beauty and mystique
Ne'er to be pulled away from one another
Playing their innocent games of hide-and-seek

Always finding him in the willow tree's leaves
While she remained undefeated every week

She was everything, reason his heart now grieves
There was no one else above or beneath her
A level all her own, toppled by life-thieves
She and his son both, now gone to the aether
His perfect family torn from their display
Only regret received from their bequeather

Yet this idiot, this Friend of No One stray
Let's his wife out of sight for weeks at a time
Instead of keeping her under castle sway?
It must be delirium staining the clime
To make the Friend think he could weave such fiction
Without our king knowing the true purpose's crime
The Friend suffers from every man's affliction
It's plain as day. She's all he's ever wanted
His sins better come with strong benediction

For white hair and red eyes keep his mind haunted
Despite pathetic attempts to throw our king
Who can see through the false wife ruse undaunted
Everyone craves her, a never-ending string
No matter how many are fought off, more come
Just endless and endless, sanity they wring!

Just then his thoughts, interrupted by a hum
Our king turns 'round, the interloper to pay
But instead greets a redhead girl from the slum

A redhead girl whose name begins with an A
    "Angel, has it been so long since we last met?
    When did I last witness those fine eyes of grey?
    But never mind that, the chest I'm sure to get
    The Friend's Twin is trying but I'm breaking her
    Slowly but surely, then we can leave this debt
    And not soon enough, I'm finished with this cur—
    Of a king, whose fat head is stuck in the clouds
    Chatter nonstop, memory an endless blur
    Desperate for a past that no longer crowds
    Unknowing of who truly sits before him
    Or the power I'll soon wield with the queen's shrouds."

Angel's quiet, engrossed as if in a hymn
So delighted to be back in his presence
Listening to him speak with vigour and vim
How did she survive back amongst the peasants?
Gone so long, too long, from our transcendent king
To return to him is one of God's presents

    "We must leave," she speaks. "Duck from the coming swing
    Step off this familiar path for your own sake
    I have to protect you from this endless ring
    One last try, please don't let it end in heartbreak
    I'm weak to begin with and grow weaker still
    Naught but a grain of sand in the desert's wake
    Leave with me, Wrenfrey, and we can break her will
    All's finally able to be put to rest
    I'm the last sliver where emptiness does fill."

Our king knows not what to do in this contest—
Of insanity and pure stupidity
So tired of this issue that's constantly pressed
Angel's words lacking any lucidity
When's it to stop, this incessant badgering?
When his body's in states of putridity?

Our king, pained, barely stops the frown gathering
      "Of course, my fair Venus. I hear your wisdom
      And thank you. Your love is truly staggering
      You'll rule well as the queen of my new kingdom
      By my side as my beautiful confidant
      The heart that beats for all, townsfolk and pilgrim
      But that can't happen if I leave nonchalant
      I do this for you just as much as for me
      The life you deserve is all I truly want."

Angel's eyes are black holes, her self absentee
Her skin cold to the touch, as if touched by Death
Sunken face like the old tales of the banshee
      "Say my name. I wish to hear it on your breath,"
Her voice falls from her, "That name which I told you
      When we first met that long night, you must sayeth."

Our king covers his sigh at this inane spew
But at least this request was much more stable
He pulls her close, hiding annoyance accrue
      "I shall say it as many times as able
      To calm your spirits and prove my devotion
      Listen, I speak it now, love, you are Angel."

Like total stillness on the open ocean
Fear of the unreal coiling around his spine
The woman in his arms, act of remotion
Blood pours from her, creature against God's design
Her hair dripping its crimson, draining with red
This vision where beauty and horror align

Our king is stock-still, body frozen in dread
Unable to fight as she pulls his face down
Her ruby lips to his, sharing the bloodshed
Can't pull back, the metallic taste like his crown—
Draws him in, pulls her closer. It's all he knows
Can't move even as he's feeling himself drown

More, he needs more of this hemorrhaging rose
A growing panic he cannot hope to fight
She tastes like his future, a future he chose
Drinking her in, in mesmerizing delight
The blood in his throat, coating all it touches
Leaving behind a singed trail as cold as night
He can't breathe, can't free himself from her clutches
Her fingers mould his skin, splitting it open
A fresh form free of humanity's crutches

More, more, more! Our king's mind finally broken
He latches onto her, thrusting forth his need
The need to take it all, destroy all hope in
This rose drenched in blood, let him fulfil his greed
Possessing, devouring in this Devil's rite
'Til naught's left but his own flesh on which to feed

Our king wakes! Safe in bed, no Angel in sight
Yet the taste of blood on his tongue does remain
Scorching his very soul with its burning bite

Not all he feels, there are eyes in his domain
Eyes not his that watch from the darkened corner
Gazing with overwhelming sadness and pain

He'll not stand for this obvious life scorner—
Invading his room! His sword will sort this out
He'll skewer this idiotic foreigner
With one quick movement, he slashes at the lout
But only met with darkness and empty air
A chill 'cross his back like a strike from a knout
Whispers not ours let our king know they're still there
But so low, so weak, the man can't comprehend

From all directions, the sadness and pain stare
Like a wave it crashes, he feels it descend
A strength of proportions even he can't fight
It pushes on him, forcing his knees to bend
Straining against the pressure, his knuckles white
Yet he can't move as it tries to tear his mind
To make the sadness his own, the pain his right

But he grits his teeth, his stubborn rage refined
Refusing to be this night's fatality
This, our king, the greatest king of humankind!

Then suddenly speech from this brutality:
    "My last attempt to push back the mind's fractures
    Return her to a sense of normality
    But it's not enough to fix heart's contractures
    Not enough, not enough, her happiness gone
    Now witness what your action manufactures."

The dark words circle Wrenfrey on the wind's yawn
Threatening to pull the muscle from the bone
Beaten by this god from unknown pantheon

Then, quick as it started, salvation is known
As the vicious wind escapes through his window
Taking the sadness and pain, him left alone

Upon hands and knees, he waits for confidence to grow
Practice for when he finds himself in the final show

CHAPTER 23

The next day, the air is different. Taut, cold
There's not much to find in the way of relief
High-pitched dirge piercing brains of all who behold
But our king on his way to the morning brief
Shakes off any force that weighs leaden and dark
Already done with the Friend and his dull grief

Our king opens the twin doors to the monarch
The Friend faces away from him, still as stone
Fire rages in the hearth, but none of warmth's spark
The Friend speaks, voice cool, "Long has our friendship grown
    So happy was I, for the chance to renew
    So much that I gave you a chance to atone
    I was pulled in, as old memories regrew
    A talent of yours or a weakness of mine?
    Persuaded to think the lost past can break through
    Memories of wrestling the castle's swine
    Of making the other laugh until sides split
    Of the three of us enjoying the sun's shine

Was it real? Were there children so closely knit?
Or do your honeyed words weave reality
Forming puppets of clay for life's counterfeit?"

He turns, his stare forever long and weighty
With a presence of betrayal, planning bloodshed
His face a frightening actuality

But our king is smooth. He stands with his arms spread
Wonder at what brought this on, but his heart knows
His mouth opens, some mitigation to thread

But the Friend cuts him off from conjuring prose,
    "My sister… it's the one thing I asked of you
    Don't touch her. But it's my own fault I suppose
    Covering for you is all my life's been through
    From husbands, fathers, now I too join the ranks
    Foolishly thinking it was me you came to."

Our king steps up. "My friend, please…" But then he blanks
As a longsword takes aim to skewer his chest

The Friend holds it. "Life I grant, you should give thanks
    You're to leave my castle, no longer my guest
    Word to spread of your profane deeds, all will hear
    A fitting punishment for all your unrest
    Throne's yours, but you're no longer a puppeteer
    Your every sighting draws irreverent whisper
    Crown on your head but power to disappear."

Our king's fists tighten. How dare this damn lisper?
He forces out a smile, friendly to the last
Ever fighting an anger that would blister
    "You are mistaken. My loyalty's steadfast
    If your sister has said something out of turn
    Trust me, my friend, I am equally aghast."

And now we get to see the Friend's dark eyes burn
    "You *fuck* my sister, then call *her* the liar?
    You foul worm, I should slice you from stem to stern!"

Our king takes a step back, too close to the fire
    "Then... then allow me a chance to say goodbye
    Let me end things, leave her not in heartbreak's mire
    Left even more forlorn, days only to cry
    As her first love is ripped from her without word
    Closure, I request, but your right to deny
    I only think of her feeling she's been spurned
    Her poor heart shattered when it could have been eased
    Let us not leave her as a broken songbird
    Yet if you still believe I'm naught but diseased
    Then cast me out, your sister forever fraught
    Or we can end this as adults, all appeased
    Please consider, my friend, a monster I'm not
    Blood brothers we were, if that means anything
    Quick goodbye, then I'm off, lesson soundly taught."

The Friend is silent. He examines our king
For a long while, it feels like an endless span

Both locked in the others' gaze, lives on a string
The sword falls away. Keeping eyes on the man
The Friend speaks, "She deserves closure, at the least
    But I'll be there, 'case this is some greater plan
    Should it be, from my vow I will be released
    No longer will I care to leave you alive
    We go now, one false move and your life is ceased."

A man at the gallows, wishing to survive
Trudged to his lover over his plan's remains
Crown shrinking from view, lest his brain can connive

The Twin's door, our king must take hold of the reins
His last chance is coming, he cannot lose it
He won't let this ruin his future campaigns
The Friend stands in the doorway, not a half-wit
As our king enters the room and is embraced
His lover, tears streaking, her whole self unfit
    "This isn't true," she cries. "A joke in poor taste
    How can this happen? We just found each other
    Please, say this is false. Let love not be erased."

Our sweet king holds her close, nearing a smother
    "It's as you fear. We've been caught and I must go
    I've done a great disservice to your brother
    And for us to part ways seems destiny's flow
    Never to see the other or feel their touch
    Not to be more in life than a cameo
    Hush now, please, your tears and sadness hurt so much."
He hugs her, his voice a whisper in her ear,

"But one thing you can do for me is to clutch—
That chest of snake and flower, pull the lid clear
I need you to unlock it. Only you can
Do this for me and do it for us, my dear."

She's confused, our king seemingly a madman
And the magnitude of his request is lost
She speaks, "Think of that no more. We need a plan
One that will free us of royalty's cruel cost
Let us both run away from this awful place
Just you and me, together 'til love's exhaust."

Our king is quiet, options losing the race
In his mind's eye, his great crown fades to nothing
His future revenge no longer has a brace
Years and years of one man's eternal planning
The things he's had to do for that stupid queen
Ash in the wind, it was truly disgusting

So our king continues his whisper routine
Into the ear of one so vulnerable
Making rationality out of obscene
His words echoing the insufferable
Riling his hate, her endless tears stain his cheek
Beads of melting gold, irrecoverable

An outside look shows lovers with future bleak
In the hushed tones, glimpses of a world unkind
Pledges of undying love to leave hearts weak

But our low voices are ghosts that trail behind
Dancing with our king's words as they crescendo
This poor girl no match for our great mastermind

The two lovers part, a last look memento
A dangerous understanding in their eyes
The end is coming with increasing tempo
Our king is then swiftly lead to his allies
Angel and the Hand wait for him at the gate
The Hand stoic, Angel unchanged in his eyes
No longer the avatar of blood and bait
Now an expression of softness and worry
Her gaze is locked on our king, a man so great!

One last time the Friend speaks, "Best if you hurry
    Back to where the Devil himself spat you out
    There's naught for you here, no goodwill to curry
    At last I see your honour, past what you tout
    It's dead as the rightful rulers of your land
    In truth, I did know, but hope was my redoubt
    That all would be as once was, the past remanned
    Once happy memories where three ran as one
    The only place for innocence to still stand
    But, at long last, you've defiled that too. Well done

    I want to ask how you could do this to me
    What you could possibly, *possibly*, have won
    But all I feel now is heartbreak for her glee
    Her eyes downcast, trying to hold hidden tears
    I doubt despair will be proved hyperbole

Your friends once, time spent as more than simple peers
Though your definition of 'friend' seems the same
As that of 'enemy'. God, the wasted years

So, Wrenfrey, when Satan calls for you by name
And you're trapped in an endless hellscape on par—
With the one you've left behind in heartless flame
When you cower before sin's horned avatar
I pray you feel our hope, the hope we carried
And it crushes you to the nothing you are."

The Friend turns on his heel, our king left harried
Our lord, his heart pounding, his fury building
He shouts, "Run to the fantasy you've married
    Tell me, what is it when a lie is childing?
    I expect an exact copy of you, *friend*!
    You say solid gold when the truth says gilding
    I know your heart's desires. It's a common trend
    You want her! They all want her! It strengthens me!
    To have what other men can only pretend
    To know I have the love and beauty of she
    Mine to the end! Mine! Mine! Mine! And never theirs!
    I'm the pinnacle of who all want to be!"

The Friend walks on, and out of our king's nightmares
Disappearing behind his guard and their arms
Not even looking back, his mind nary cares
Leaving our majestic king huffing his charms
Only ending his eloquent argument—
When Angel placed a hand to calm the alarms

He turns his gaze back, the wildness permanent
He grows tired of this game that never ceases
His rage strong enough to pierce the firmament

But soon our king won't be the only one in pieces
Any minute now when sweet hell truly releases

CHAPTER 24

The walk back to the queen, an infinite trudge
Failures, their quarry forever out of reach
The Majesty proven right her right to judge

Damned if he returns on his knees to beseech
Our self-righteous king won't beg her forgiveness
Two other objectives, he completed each
More than enough time given, her Hand witness
Her men require a man of substance to lead
No doubt they're itching for victory's richness
Warriors live on blood, violence their need
Our king can convince them he's the better choice
War of revenge will compel their bloody greed

Beside him, the red-haired serf can't find her voice
As they cross the threshold of the queen's castle
She is silent, downcast, devoid of rejoice
The Hand sweeping them along without hassle
Titan leading them through the halls of his queen

The ex-king lower than the lowest vassal
Whose perceptive eyes catch something so obscene
Tapestries of violet hang on the stone
The crest of his house, like a stab in the spleen
Does this queen mock him? Enjoy the chaos sown?
Without another thought, our king marches past
Moving by the Hand, the doors to the side, blown
Revealing the queen's throne room, the space still vast
His prior deeds, in a blanket on the ground
The Majesty unmoved from her seat, steadfast

Our king stands before her, audacity found
Cool and collected versus irate and vexed
Our king's patience thin, he's been endlessly wound
He speaks, "Why do I feel all this a pretext—
    To see me flounder, cry, grovel at your feet?
    No true success to find, my revenge you've hexed
    Like the other kings, but not nearly as sweet
    They turned me away while you play with your food!
    I may've failed, but I refuse to further bleat."

No words from the queen, but quickly comes her brood
The Hand, Angel in tow, enters the conflict
Titan, their mouthpiece, "Ignore his attitude
    There is more at work here than he can predict
    Such narrowed vision and single-minded thought—
    Will never evolve past the pain it'll inflict
    And pain it did, pain to last past what's first wrought
    As it spreads, infects all around like disease
    Once again, he proves his lust for the distraught."

The queen gives a pregnant pause, enough to tease
Before her soul-destroying voice joins the fray
    "You say you failed, fallen king, you're ill at ease
    Yet I see the fruits of your labour this day."

The queen's hand a shadow, then in it a form
The Twin's chest! The lid closed but lock fell away
The queen speaks, "It arrived first, bucking the norm
    With a note, a sonnet for you, fallen king
    Allow me the pleasure, aloud to inform..."

Dearest Wrenfrey,

How can I compare to those in your grace?
Always the little girl on the outside
Her heart aflutter each look at your face
Never to be the one who's called your bride

Until that fateful night you embraced me
Tangled in the others' truest passion
I felt it, our union was meant to be
Only destroyed by lack of compassion

But you sang me a song of requital
Peace found not in this life but in the next
A knife at my side, ready and vital
I await you, love, no longer perplexed

As I take my life, I take it for you
As you promised to take yours, our love true

Always,
Your Forever

"...Thus ends the loving letter of your plaything,"
The queen's screeching voice is almost sorrowful
If it weren't for the void she's embodying
    "The chest given, its owner blind from love's pull
    Congratulations, the eleventh hour
    Over all eyes, you're able to wrap your wool
    Soon you'll have what you earned, the sweet and dour
    But at what cost? Did you care to think of that?
    No, such are the gifts of royalty's power."

Our king's in shock, never thought trimming the fat—
Was the answer. What a useful little girl!
His luck returning, victory to get at
He speaks, "Then, beautiful queen, time to unfurl
    Our plans for domination of our rival
    All three tasks lie complete to defeat the churl
    Thanks to my brilliance, compose my revival
    Use your magicks to orchestrate what needs be
    Your men ensuring my birthright's survival
    For so long I was forced amongst the beastly
    Creatures barely human, rolling in their filth
    Their minds unfit to a startling degree
    Now so close, oh please, let the contents be spilth
    The contract fulfilled, my crown reinstated
    So I need not return to the land of tilth."

      "As you wish."

The queen's hand pulls back the lid, long awaited
And out comes a ball of pure light, a new star
Angelic in form, innocence created
So small, but its journey, it need not go far
Floating down between them all to the bottom
To the blanket stuffed full with a sight to scar
Gyrating offal and the bones that sought them
Wait patiently for the final puzzle piece
Our king with the obligations that caught him

He watches as the light enters life's new lease
Enveloped by the pulsating organ mess
And tiny bones hidden in the blanket fleece

Silence follows, comfortable as an abscess
Anticipation, annoyance, impatience
It takes all our favourite king can possess
Finished with all these orders of obeisance
His time as this throne room's jester is done with
Even though the queen's stare demands complacence

As our king steps up, the eloquent wordsmith
Sudden noise threatens the throne room asunder
A devilish sound like a creature from myth

A familiar sound, of blubbering blunder
The cry! A baby! Formed from the parts amassed
Small arms wiggle, eyes dart, each sight a wonder

This... this is what our king... he was flabbergast
A useless sack of flesh! He risked life and limb!
A joke! What indignity is further asked?

Cries rock the room, Angel controlled by her whim
She runs to the false promise to hold him close
Cooing at him, rocking him, humming a hymn
The most beautiful baby boy, head to toes
Her heart is overcome, her need to cherish
So strong her love, one only a mother knows

But sudden explosions! All turns nightmarish!
Another follows! Then a third! Fourth and fifth!
Wood and stone come way! In fire, senses perish!

Angel clutches the babe, our king steps forthwith
Eerie calm of the queen, demeanour unchanged
Over the blasts, he shouts to the monolith,
 "What's going on? What foul plot has been arranged?
 I demand the meaning of this. Tell me now!
 What are these quakes, shaking your core 'til deranged?"

Slowly, deathly, the queen rises, putrid sow
Each step punctuated with a voice from Hell
 "It is what you wished for: the war from your vow."

Another step closer, another quake's knell
 "Krios lies just outside, trebuchets ready
 Anger, heartbreak in his breast he'll never quell."

Towards our king, gait ethereal, steady
    "It appears he found his sister, her wrists slit
    Drenched in her own blood. His sanity thready."

Our king's heart beats, each a pulverizing hit
As the queen stands before him, a breath between
    "Her note left echoes a certain hypocrite
    Promises to go together, he could glean
    He's here to ensure you live up to that pledge
    Dear. Fallen. King," ends the taunting of the queen

Our king's sanity walks on a razor's edge
Each quake a hammer to his skull as fires build
He's falling, fingers can't grasp asylum's ledge
She's in front of him, the awakening chilled
The shadows swaying around the pale queen's face
Each beat of his heart matching their dance fulfilled
A final darkness none can hope to erase
His coarse words barely make it out, "Who are you?"

Dry is his throat as shadows move and displace
Sight of crimson over deathly white run through
Mutilated grin straining from ear to ear
Screams of agony trapped behind, where hate grew

Our king stumbles back, but it won't disappear
The repulsive grin of blood, with scorn to match
The eyes of anathema, his puppeteer

Our king's trembling hand finds Angel's to latch
He pulls her away from the sight of horror
They have inevitability to catch

Oh, let fear wash your meat 'round every corner
Each step away brings us closer together
You realize Satan acts as your scorer?

The cries of the babe loosen his mind's tether
The quakes of the castle, attacked, breaks spirit
Fires raging, scenes pulled from Lucifer's nether

The trio run away. They can still clear it!
Down halls, servants of shroud watch them, unmoving
Angel's weeping but he can scarcely hear it
Screams from outside are sanity-removing
Piercing his head, flooding him, chaos abound
Smoke, exhaustion, making all things confusing

Quick! To the hidden passage, before they're found!
To safety it will lead them, far from this point
But in our cackles, our poor king's mind is drowned
And at his back he feels her, set to anoint
Send our king on his way. It's time for our feast!
Ne'er full we are! Ready for flesh, blood, and joint!

The crying continues, the babe's wrath released
Yes, yes, yes, little pest! You too want him caught
Show us! With each step, let your screams be increased

Inferno greets them. The secret entrance fraught
But her gaze is on you, our king, burning cold
Now drag your lover through what arrogance wrought

Footsteps echo through. Our king tightens his hold
Ignoring her cries of pain, 'else be deceased
Faster! In the distance, he hears his bells tolled!

Our poor king is losing the man to the beast
His eyes tunnelling, mouth frothing, lungs heaving
But it all tastes the same to our tongues, at least

Then a crack above! Wooden supports cleaving!
Down comes the stone and wood, Angel and our king—
On separate sides, a small gap for perceiving
No way over, no way 'round, and she's coming

Our king turns to Angel, then to freedom's call
She and the babe trapped, left to deal with that thing
Or the light in the distance, end of the hall
Nary a question, he takes a step away
Our king's at rock-bottom, nowhere else to fall

But lo! He finds himself unable to stray!
Sting of conscience or love stronger than first thought?

Ha! A hand grips his wrist, prolonging his stay
Angel reaches through the gap, wood burning hot
Her strength unparalleled, fingers gouge his skin

Determined not to let go of what she sought
    "Don't leave us, Wrenfrey!" she calls, terror her kin

But the cold heat of *her* gaze is growing near
They'll all be consumed by these creatures of sin
He grabs Angel's arm, want to wrench himself clear
He has to get free, evil is arriving
Our bold king must save that which he holds most dear

Yanking, twisting, pulling, panic is thriving
The pale hand maintains its herculean grip
Tearing, clawing, biting, coward reviving

    "Let go, you fucking bitch!" our brave king lets slip

But this angel's of the divine, so's her love
Her strength stays, determination ne'er to skip

She speaks through tears, "The babe, he'll fit if I shove!
    Let him survive this reckoning not his own
    Please! He's just a baby! Oh, Father above
    Save him, Frey! Allow him the chance to get grown
    Please, please, please, I'm begging you, offer my soul!
    Just take him. You can't run to safety alone

        Don't let my son die here!"

But blinding dread has taken our king's mind whole
From his boot, a knife, with which he lashes out

Cutting, stabbing, but can't accomplish his goal
Drenched in blood, pale arm painted, remains devout—
To its purpose of keeping our king in place
No escape, and a choice is made with no doubt

Reaching through the gap, hard with so little space
The baby's cries piercing, with no antidote
Angel to her lover with a hopeful face

Our chivalrous King Wrenfrey slits her pale throat

Ear to ear, a smile of hanging flesh and blood
Still, as though what happened was nothing of note
Her gaze captured in his, holding up this bud
As if their gaze capable of freezing time
All is picturesque before the coming flood
Fantasy bleeding from reality's crime
Hair of white shock, eyes match arterial spray
As the illusion finds a suitable rhyme

But our king's eyes drop and the spell falls away
Angel releases him to grab at her wound
As crimson seeps, free at last to disobey

Then he's gone. His honour once merely harpooned—
Now absolutely forgotten, left to die
On an island of his own make, it's marooned
Totally alone to stare up at the sky

Not a ship in sight to save it from this land
Yet still blind, calling out to the cruel world: "Why?"

Why must Frey suffer? Languish in flames the Devil's fanned?
And perhaps it would answer, if not slain by his hand

CHAPTER 25

Screams, only screams as he exits the tunnel
All around him, soldiers of his rival march
Onto their swords where the peasantry funnel
Slash through a woman forming a crimson arch
Stab through a man to make a whirlwind of red
Always more so their bloodlust will never parch

No fault of theirs, the circumstances that led—
Both sides to demise, the consequence of one
Our king why the roads are littered with the dead
The dead he spares not one single glance for, none
But to hide among them as the army roams
Scouring the streets of the kingdom their side's won
A hand reaches for our king from rubbled homes
    "Help us, please, help us…" a frail voice whispers out

Trapped in this cold kingdom's growing catacombs
Our king reels back, away from the dying lout
Only to feel the chill of death on his neck
And another voice cuts through his panicked shout

"Save us, king…" a shade, her arms reach, her hands beck

A shrouded servant but the shroud falls away
Skeletal, charred, evil close enough to peck
More and more approach, their bodies of decay
Shrieking, grasping demons the Old Son has made
Withered omens of death, creatures of doomsday
Our king's brain is boiling, senses start to fade
Survive, his goal, it's only ever been so
His life, his bloodline, his pride and accolade
He must flee these hollow shepherds from below
He'll start over, start fresh, a new wife and child

Quickly, 'fore he ends up food for worm and crow!
Skeletal abominations, sight reviled
They stalk closer in unholy abandon
Wish to stain with hands of the Heaven-exiled

Our king recoils from them, his feet in tandem
Racing, racing, over the fields of deceased
His freedom worth all the gold and platinum
But where's our king to go to hide from the Beast?
The willow! The one from their childhood stories
It shields against evil well as any priest
It's the only chance for his noble glories
A reprieve from the darkness to find God's word
Wait for normalcy in the territories

Behind our king, the thunder of boots is heard
Dive into the willow, hide amongst its leaves

Quiet now, your pursuers are undeterred
Their shouts and screams are what Lucifer achieves
Circling 'round our king, around and around
Like demons set loose on the mortal's reprieves
Our king is safe, this willow on holy ground
Saves those with good hearts, paragons of their kind
Hidden from the deceitful and the Hell-bound
And our king's the best of the best God's designed
No way or how evil can hope to find him
Even as their wailing tries to break his mind

Then all goes quiet, all at once, growing grim
The stomping stops, the shrieks, howls, cries, it all ends
Left is our king and the shaking in each limb

"We see you, Wrenfrey."

His heart stops, the last sliver of sense suspends
No, no, no! He's safe. He's safe from evil here!
She can't see him, do what dark desire intends
She speaks, "Come see the kingdom you hold so dear
    Yet abandon at earliest convenience
    The kingdom you placed on the tip of a spear
    Come out, Wrenfrey, beg each for our lenience
    Come out, Wrenfrey, and face what your greed has wrought
    Or we'll come in, to make proper acquaintance."

Our king's feet remain planted, his muscles taut
His eyes focused on the light between the leaves
And when they shift, he's brave as an argonaut

In comes four of the Hand, mission of retrieves
Our king screams, "No! Get away from me! No! No!
    I'll... I'll pay you, whatever your heart conceives!"

But there is nothing our poor king can bestow
That he himself hasn't already destroyed
So they each grab a limb, haul him like cargo
Our king fights, on his way to who they're employed
She of cold fire, ghost appearance, heart of stone
No, not of stone. Her heart's replaced with black void

Beyond, eyes watch this unfold, eyes not his own
Eyes filled with overwhelming sadness and pain
Eyes of a woman ne'er seen but presence known
Hunched, weight of the world causes her shoulders' strain
Irises of black jasper, deep like the night
With deep-set wrinkles that only the wise gain

The wind picks up her braids, revealing a sight
Her head tilts to one side, her neck ripped, flesh torn
There, unmistakable burns from a rope's bite
Then her body falls away to leaf and thorn
A soul freed of its case but never to leave
The wind in the weeping willow left to mourn

But our king's attention's called, the Hand to heave—
Their putrid duty upon the wretched ground
Our king in shambles, no more tricks up his sleeve

                "Wrenfrey, look at me."

The familiar voice of a wife and queen crowned
The familiar voice of a young girl, a friend
The familiar voice of a creature unbound

All twisting upon the other to no end
Old memories wheezing through that grotesque smile
Where guilt, betrayal, and anger all descend

Against his will, his eyes rise to the trial
To be drowned in the blood of her ruby gaze
There's no hope, no love, no wish to reconcile
Just her, a beast of a thousand mouths to raze
Rows and rows of sharp teeth eager for his guilt
Madness at vision's edge 'til the end of days

Flanked by Titan, a mountain of a man built
Her slave, her friend, trapped forever by her side
A soul of sorrow, honour never to tilt
He'll not leave her, his afterlife he's denied
He feels responsible for all of her pain
He swears himself to her 'til justice applied
For now, he's a watcher as she sets her feign
Stacking all the pieces, setting up the stage
And then doing it all, all over again

"Wrenfrey…" comes her voice, a voice no one can gauge

Our king before her, down on all fours, how sad
A monster that only belongs in a cage
She speaks, "How long until all of us go mad?

Or are we there, bathing in shared lunacy?
Our rationality chipped at with a gad?
Leaving not even one speck of fluency
And unable to see with wide-open eyes
Left to the crows and worms, fighting uselessly

So's the tale of one girl you should memorize
Who's mind and heart were so terribly at odds
She sloughed off a second half to vocalize
One believed in justice over he who lauds
While the other knew there was still good in him
And would not believe that memory defrauds

She remembered the boy with vigour and vim
Who read to his friends stories of Greek pagans
The look upon his face, joy filled to the brim
A child's abandon, bliss pure and unshaken
Speaking with such delight, a beacon of light
And the girl knew then that her heart was taken

So when disaster struck them, her man the blight
She begged a chance to save him, to save his soul
To prove his integrity, to set things right
The other half relented, would act the role
Using the souls from those previously wronged
They made their own story that they could control

The loving half, oh what her loving had spawned
Trying to convince her love to turn away
Yet it merely showed it was her death prolonged

But she would not give up, would not go astray
If she failed once, twice, thrice, she would try again
To prove the boy was still there, lively and gay

But with every attempt she herself would drain
She held on, reminding herself of her goal
Her weakening hands clutching the awful pain
She'd do it for him, let it consume her whole
Even as all was swept up in disarray
Whatever was needed, she would pay the toll

So she tried and tried, but his path did not sway
Growing weaker, her own memory fading
'Til she was just another one in their play
A shell with no mind to their masquerading
No personality beyond want to help
And no name, forgotten in her crusading

So she was pulled along like a common whelp
To experience what the two halves laid out
Compliant, uttering not a single yelp
But the other half was always thereabout
There when a friend said her husband had turned crazed
There when she was surprised by her lack of doubt

And of course, there when the only son she raised—
Died in her arms when his father slit her throat
Leaving them, without one look back, to be razed."

The queen's voice stops, emotionless end-of-quote
Its weight hangs in the air, cradled by the wind
Our savoury king can barely keep afloat
His mouth falls open, his pride finally thinned
He blubbers like a babe, like the son he killed
    "I'm sorry… please forgive me for I have sinned
    And let it be known your revenge is fulfilled
    I have seen what's been done, you've been offended
    I lie prostrate before you, you should be thrilled
    The error of my ways I've learned—amended!
    It's a new man you see, a more gentle man
    Let's leave the rest of this tale open-ended

    I'll retire to a farm, humility's plan
    In truth, it's the life I wanted all along
    And we'll never meet again in this lifespan."

He's answered by silence, the feeling of wrong
The Hand stands around him, still and foreboding
Air around him is dead, empty of birdsong
The queen cradles his face, patience eroding
Looking down at him with her piercing rose glare
Soft pale hands on his cheeks, the touch corroding
In her deathly, hollow voice, constant nightmare
    "My neck slit from ear to ear, I stumble back
    Sliding down the wall in shock and deep despair
    My throat gushing bright crimson from the attack
    I hear the cries of my son pressed to my breast
    He's drenched in my blood but my arms do not slack

The disorientation keeps my grip stressed
Even as blood starts to fill his mouth and nose

His cries become gurgles, terror manifest
My vision wanes, crawling in creeping shadows
My only wish to die fast, so he'll be freed
But I don't. I feel his struggle 'til it slows

His hand touches mine, face desperate with need
Equals my desperation to see him free
Yet I can do naught but continue to bleed
Then, I hear my son's final gasp, his last plea
Drowned in his mother's blood by his father's sin
Never knowing the man he was meant to be
Future stolen, legacy ne'er to begin
Now reduced to a sack of death to decay
His last sight to be his mother's bloody grin."

The queen leans in close, her voice does not betray—
Whatever swirl of emotion rests inside
It's a cold whisper. "You killed my son, Wrenfrey."

Our delectable king, there's nowhere to hide
Adrenaline only further salts your meat
As you kneel before her, slack-jawed and tongue-tied
Your voice is layered with a panic so sweet,
    "Another chance! You say this is not the first
    That this is a cycle destined to repeat
    Our endless loop in which you are so well-versed

Throw me back to feral wolves of poverty
This time I shall see your opinion reversed."

Our king can use her fool's generosity—
To discern this place, take the crown from her head
Then all will be set right in the monarchy

"No."

Our king blinks, his colour draining, "But you said—"

She speaks, "Chances laid with the half who loved you
Yet time and again you left that half for dead
To grow weaker, hollow, with each new debut
Now a ghost, a fleeting memory of yore
Dear, there's no one left for you to appeal to

You're mine, Wrenfrey."

Our king's voice cuts off, unable to implore
As around his throat, a thick rope ties a noose
His destiny he can no longer ignore

He's yanked backwards, struggling, but it's no use
On the other end is the weight of his crimes
With all finally free of the puerile truce

Dragged through the dirt his very presence begrimes
Each sharp tug pulling him closer and closer
Back to the willow, revenge at long last chimes

Our king to the queen, his terror he shows her
Clawing at his neck, tears in his bloodshot eyes
Pathetic to justice's grandest composer
The composer who speaks past his useless cries,

    "Lay in a bed of your own making, Wrenfrey

    For not one action led you here, not one lie

    But multiple, o'er the course of life's decay

    Victims left in your uncaring, prideful wake

    Strangers, friends, loves, brothers, parents you betray

    A woman's house burned to ash on rumour's sake

    Her only crimes being a matron of herbs

    And having what's desired by a future rake

    Such sadness and pain encroaches and perturbs

    To find her adopted daughter, she sought aid

    But to regular folk her presence disturbs

    Frustrated by lacking justice, her Sons strayed

    To find who was responsible, to find you

    And their answers came in the form of a blade

    Your guards struck them down, from their hearts steel withdrew

    And the matron was alone with heartbreak's pang

    So she freed her saddened self with a noose's view

    It is she who's the willow from which you hang

    The weeping willow who weeps for her children

    Her Sons and daughter remade with claw and fang

    Now, 'round your neck is a rope of hair golden

    Once a proud queen's with her own promising sons

Just to lose everything when one turned villain
The boy she treasured, love and gifts in the tons
You wanted for nothing. She made sure of that
As loving eyes stare into your empty ones
But everything was not enough for this brat
Like the gods from your Greek stories and fables
You demanded both the choice meat and the fat
With your ambitions set on royal labels

You searched for an exploit, a switching of sons
The wicked kind nobility enables
You poisoned your brother and through your sword runs
Through his chest to join your father in death's grasp
But on that day, their deaths weren't your only ones
The Queen, your dear mother, heard madness' cold rasp
She wished a climb to Heaven, so she took one
Plummeting down instead to terrified gasps

But your last achievement, yourself you've outdone
To teach a lesson, prove your supremacy
You used a girl's heart in a game to be won
False affections leading before ecstasy
Hollow whispers of love twisting love's longing

Each meeting you shed virtue like leprosy
Leaving behind an imprint of your wronging
As you took advantage of her diffidence
A seduction of hate and ego thronging
What end laid for perversion of innocence?
When its belly swelled with sinful pregnancy?

Yet she was not the target of recompense
A malefactor driven by jealousy
To hurt your closest friend, your brother by choice
You get to feel the strength of that legacy
For she is the weight, keeping you from rejoice
Holding you down, your veins as stone, your blood lead
Chokes and hacks and coughs are now your only voice."

Our king yanked higher and higher overhead
His lungs have lost all breath, and with it his screams
Impossible pain coils, through his body spread

On the other end, zealots of their queen's schemes
Pull tight the rope, each draw with finality
The Hand, her hand, key that no longer redeems

Each wrenching jerk they make to totality
There's no compassion from our king's once allies
Summoned to demonstrate their brutality
Capillaries bursting inside our king's eyes
Tears of blood, tongue swells as his clenching teeth crack
His lungs caustic ash. They're ripping from their tie
His heart beats erratic, vision spots of black
As inside, his arteries pump thick dead sludge
And his organs are on to ruin and wrack

He sees forms, the Witch's Sons, strength in their grudge
Shadowed by two, King father and Heir brother
Another pull of the rope, all act as judge

Then more faces, the Witch and his Queen mother
They heave his body with their grips on the rope
With the Twin and a certain grey-eyed other

The Angel, crimson-haired, with thoughts to elope
Now an empty shell, she joins her family
Her eyes cold, his victims, filled with long dead hope

But there's more to join in our king's agony
A boy and a young swain with an older gent
They pull the rope the hardest, this tragedy
With eyes of the soulless, sanity segment
Twisted grins and sharpened horns, forked tongue slithers
A gaze where humanity does not frequent

They are him, his mirrored reflections with hers
How the rest see him, as a monstrosity
Where any chance of deliverance withers
But soon comes the desired tortuosity
Titan to hammer the rope into the ground
Each hit preserves picturesque atrocity
Each slam pulses to where our king is now bound
High above them, his new throne from which to rule
A kingdom worthy of him finally found

Darkened fog, acidic smoke, black shadows duel
As the queen glides to him, her face takes his view
Eye to eye, she looks upon him, her voice cool
    "End of your story, but not the end of you
    For every second my babe son should have lived

A lifetime shall pass. Days, months, years to accrue
No pleas for pity, no excuses to give
Just the endless void, never to be rid of
Mercy your water, but find your hands a sieve
Behold, this is my curse on you: life, *my love*
Forever, an eternity your domain
Nothingness, no Devil or Father above
Just you on this infinitely stretching plane
With the one person who always loved you most."

With that, she holds up the symbol of his reign
His crown! The gold, the jewels he so loved to boast
But in the gold, in the jewels, his reflection
A thousand stare back at him, back at their host

Crimson pours from their eyes like an infection
Claw marks cover their necks as their tongues protrude
Foam dribbling past their lips' pale complexion
A hand's width from him, what he so long pursued
If he could reach out, if he could just grab hold

But his arms stay at his sides, ever subdued
Left to his own staring gaze, trapped in the gold
Caged in a prison of ruby and sapphire
A captive to something unloving and cold

Then it cracks. The jewels fall into the quagmire
Collapsing in on itself, his stares follow
'Til all's left is dust for the wind to inspire

Left in its wake, no emotions to wallow
The queen, babe at her breast, Titan at her side
This is the last she'll speak to our Apollo
    "A final look at what your ego denied
    Perhaps you'll gain true understanding, shame sought
    Perhaps you won't, and stay feeling justified
    Truth be told, I care not if a lesson's taught
    My goal was never rehabilitation
    But to see the look on your face, the beast caught
    Your look at your final ramification
    We leave you behind, the pride you've begotten
    To dwindle from the mind, an expurgation
    Your legacy erased, memory rotten
    Never again to be in anyone's thoughts
    Just totally and utterly forgotten

    Goodbye, Wrenfrey."

Our king can't scream, can't shout, attempts lead to naughts
He watches them disappear, Titan, his son
His wife, white hair flows through his vision's black spots

Then they are gone, their roles in this story done
Leaving no evidence of their existence
And our great king is ours, we've finally won

    "Wrenfrey, our Wrenfrey," we sing, closing distance

Our devotion to him across the expanse
His body our reward for our persistence

His meat on display, such a seductive dance
Sing with us, our king, our love at last released
Surely there's a tune for this divine romance

As we wriggle from the dirt, our patience ceased
As we fly in on our black wings, salivating
As we buzz around your head, eager to feast
We climb your legs, smell of meat permeating
We crawl over your body, tender and fresh
We land on your shoulders, control abating

We thank you for sharing, this boon we enmesh
Skin destined to regrow, muscles to reknit
What a gift, this source of never-ending flesh
By her words, soul and body will ne'er be split
You'll feed us, bellies to swell with autocrat
How kind, this unending banquet you permit
To grow strong on your strength, grow fat on your fat

See the delight you've fostered in us, our king
From the murder of crows to the smallest gnat
You hurried to us as quick as legs would bring
Knowing we hungered for body and spirit
You care for us so much, your love is wellspring

Your loyal subjects, to your great presence we submit!
Now, if we may, abydocomist's our favourite

EPILOGUE

A whirlwind of activity seconds long
Then nothing as the whole forest goes quiet
A hunt, a fight between the quick and the strong

Evidence in the air of a wolf's diet
Fresh flesh, gurgled gasps, gnashing fangs, blood-soaked maw
Beast with their prize, daring any to try it
Prey's eyes darting as it is devoured raw
Still beating crimson from wounds, adding to taste
Too weak to scream but too strong for life's withdraw
The wolf is ravenous, but will it be waste?
Vigour drops away from its protruding ribs
Its mind is crazed with the hunger that it's faced
As it gnaws on its meal's own protruding ribs
Both see the other as foe, as brief life's scare
The wolf sees the prey's grass, fields with endless bids
While they with sharpened fangs must choose food with care
Prey too strong? Hurt. Prey too small? Not much to eat
Wait too long? Prey eats the grass your corpse'll prepare

Jealousy brews between predator and meat
If only their lives were given the same gifts
Instead, a thankless one was their bloody treat

But they are not alone in their 'only ifs'
Prey sees themselves as never having a chance
Amongst those whose supremacy never shifts

They must fear all, adrenaline in their stance
Attention left, right, ears perked for the discreet
Fatalities often come with one missed glance

Jealousy brews between the fair and the cheat
If only their lives were given the same skill
Instead, a thankless one was their bloody treat

Moribund predator and moribund kill
The wolf's weak jaws gumming, its meal came too late
Last of its vitality lost in hunt's thrill
Thoughts of their survival begin to abate
Die of starvation with a mouth full of food
Until together, both their wills dissipate

Only to be found by a curious brood
Three children, one bright girl and two handsome boys
Coming across such brutality conclude

One boy pokes the wolf with a sickening noise
Cackling as the other boy holds back sick
And mocking the weakness in his lack of poise

But it is the weak boy who feels something slick
Up against his neck, the girl's crying eyes press
Sadness from the extinguishing of life's wick
And the first boy feels something he can't express
Watching her with him, picking him for support
His chest tightens over her choice of noblesse

It's ugly, this feeling, makes his thoughts distort
A turning in his stomach, filled with thick oil
Ne'er before had his frustrations been so short

A whole mess of memories inside him boil
Always second choice, even in his own home
Always, always, always! Insides twist and roil

Why never him? His thoughts beginning to roam
The hand 'round the stick gets tighter and tighter
With the building of this mystery syndrome

What's wrong with him? What's this hate-filled igniter?
He forces himself to drop what's in his hand
He's an intellectual, not a fighter

And so he tells stories from the pagan land
His friends' eyes growing wide, enthralled by his tales
Once again, the centre of their merry band
And as the girl moves closer, his plan unveils
He links an arm 'round hers, then the other boy

Puts himself between the two to fix what ails
Unknowingly, the fabled Greek horse for Troy
Smile on the outside but inside darkness grows
Unaware even to him, it'll coat each joy

Who would have thought that a simple day's walk would impose—
On the rest of a boy's life, forever in shadows

ABOUT
KAILIE MARIE LYNN BILL

Kailie Marie Lynn Bill is a Canadian-born author who discovered her love of writing at a very early age. Her extensive travels and diverse life experiences have nurtured her passion for storytelling, each serving as inspiration for her craft. And, despite loving the art of writing and spending decades on different projects, penning this bio was definitely the hardest thing she's ever had to do.

For more by Kailie Marie Lynn Bill, check out her website: kailiebill.com